Fractal Fun
a grayscale coloring book for adults

Hannah Moesker

ISBN: 1541067681
ISBN-13: 978-1541067684

INTRODUCTION

When using a fractal program, which is based on mathematical equation, and changing variables like color and depth you will get a piece of art that is one of a kind.

This book will enable you to achieve professional looking colorings as all of the shading is provided for you in these fractal illustrations.
These are grayscale images, not traditional black and white line art coloring pages.
Each grayscale fractal has been modified to get a soft, velvet and sophisticated feeling.

Grayscale coloring for adults is one of the newest trends in adult coloring and is rapidly increasing in popularity. It gives you a solid base to start coloring, without worrying about the light and dark parts.

Each page is printed on one side, so you can remove it for framing or gifts. Great for colored pencils and gel pens.
Markers will bleed through and need an extra piece of absorbing paper (blotter paper) underneath the coloring page.
If you like to use card stock or another type of paper, you are welcome to copy the coloring pages, for your personal use only.

Exploring the fractal coloring pages in depth and working your magic with colored pencils, gel pens or other tools you like, will bring you joy, relaxation and many 'feel good' hours.
It is my hope that you will enjoy the world of fractals, color and motion and happily walk hand in hand with me

**along the way,
to color the gray.**

What will you get:

- Large size coloring book at 8.5" x 11" (21 x 29 cm)
- 30 single-sided grayscale pages AND a bonus of 4 postcards 6" x 4.5" to make as gifts! These are the only double printed pages, because of the postcard template at the backsite. So please, be careful to use materials that tend to bleed through
- High-quality - Matte cover professional finish
- Gel pen, pastel chalk, and colored pencil friendly
- Perfect for relaxation, color therapy and art therapy

Hannah Moesker

TESTING YOUR MATERIALS

Here you can test your various tools on how they react with some of the grayscale colors.

Please note that the darker colored squares are harder to color with lightly tinted colored pencils.

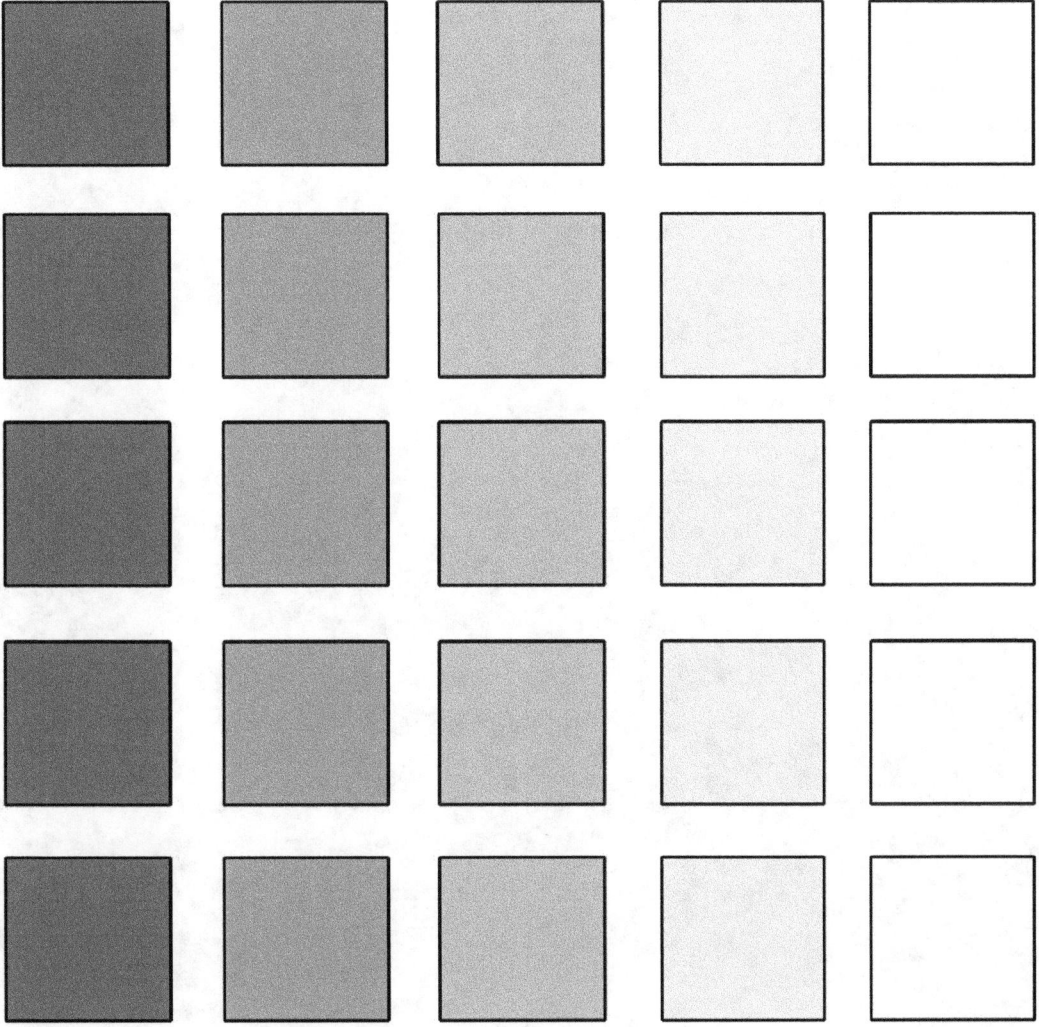

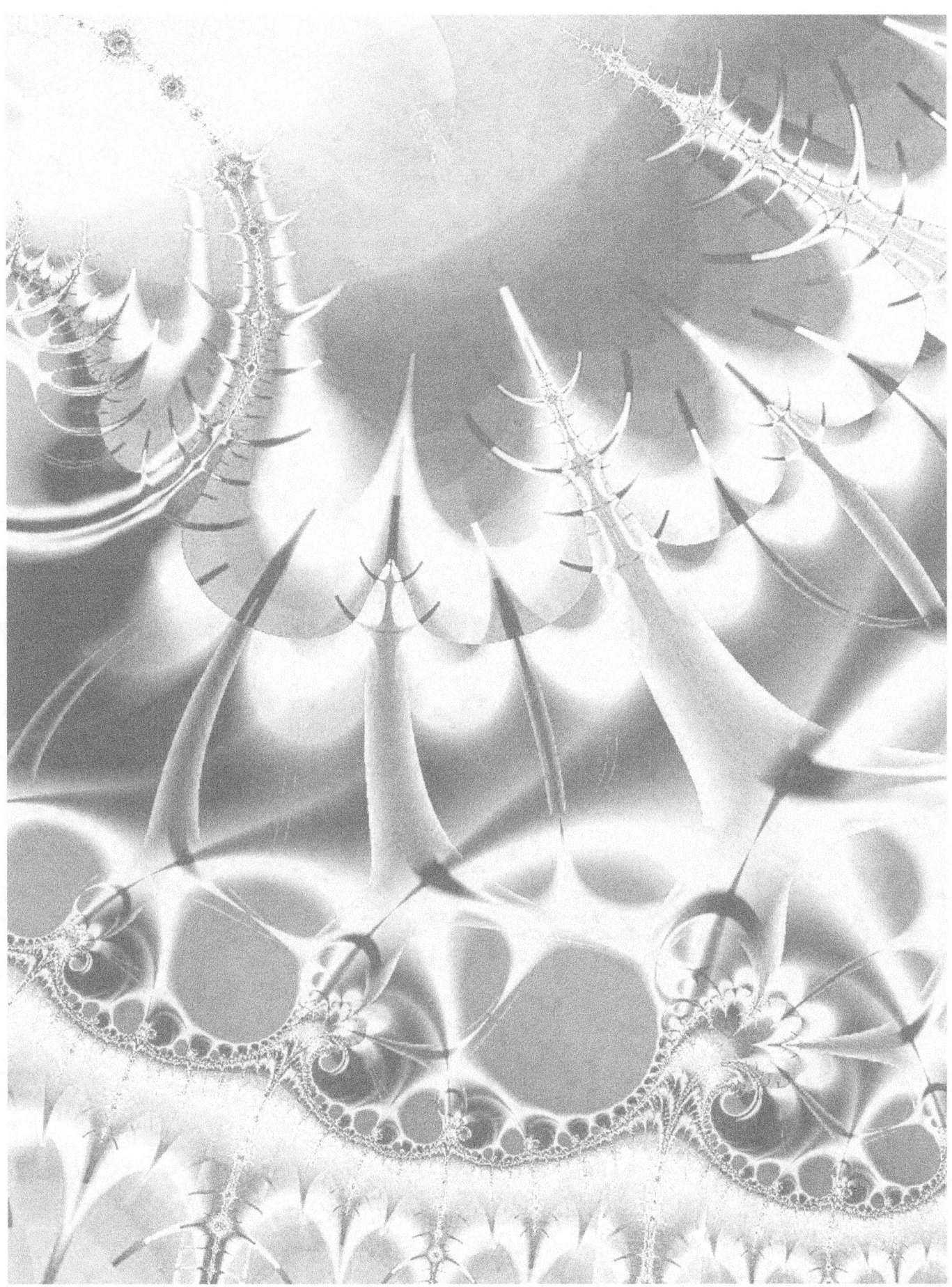

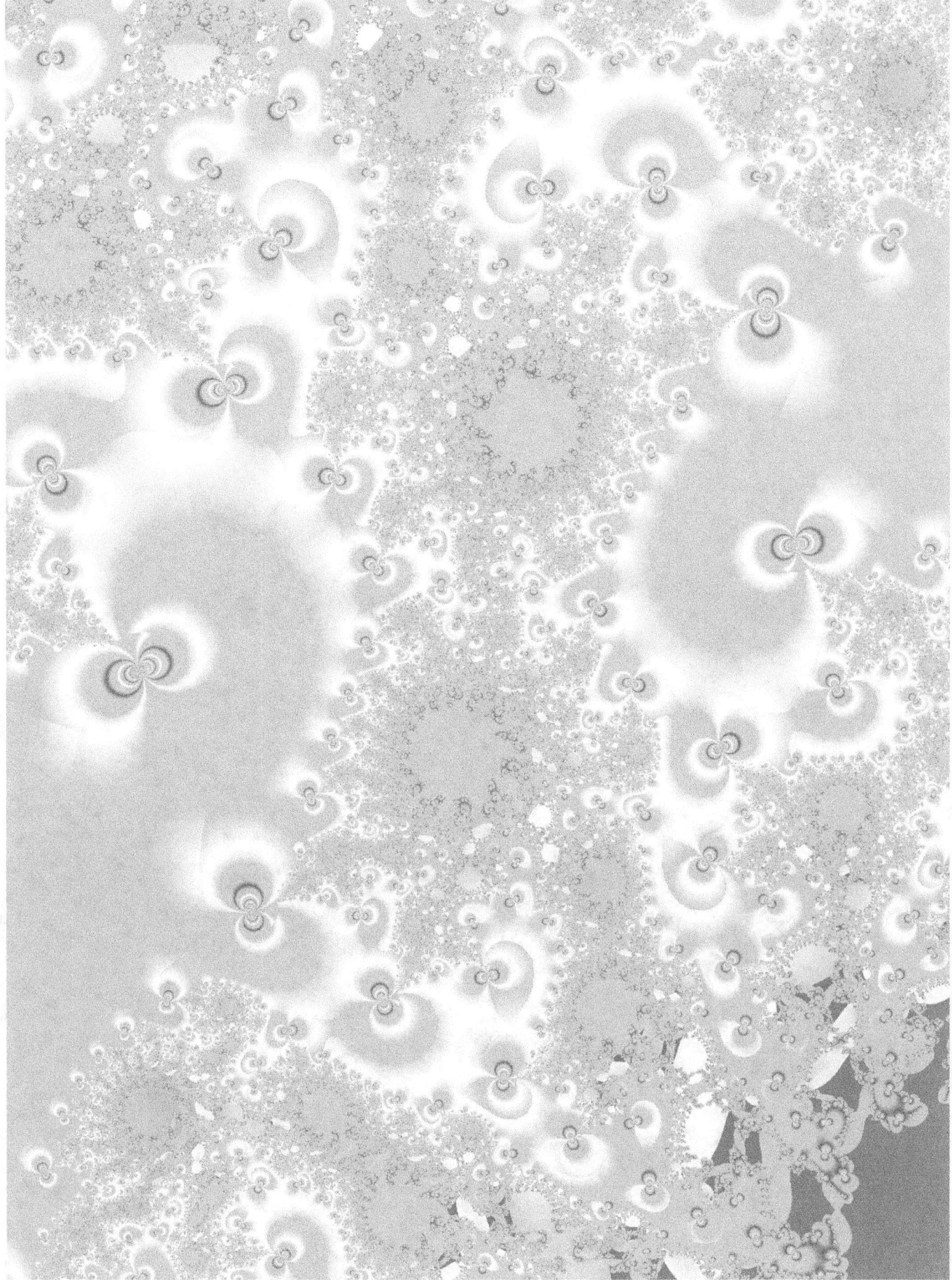

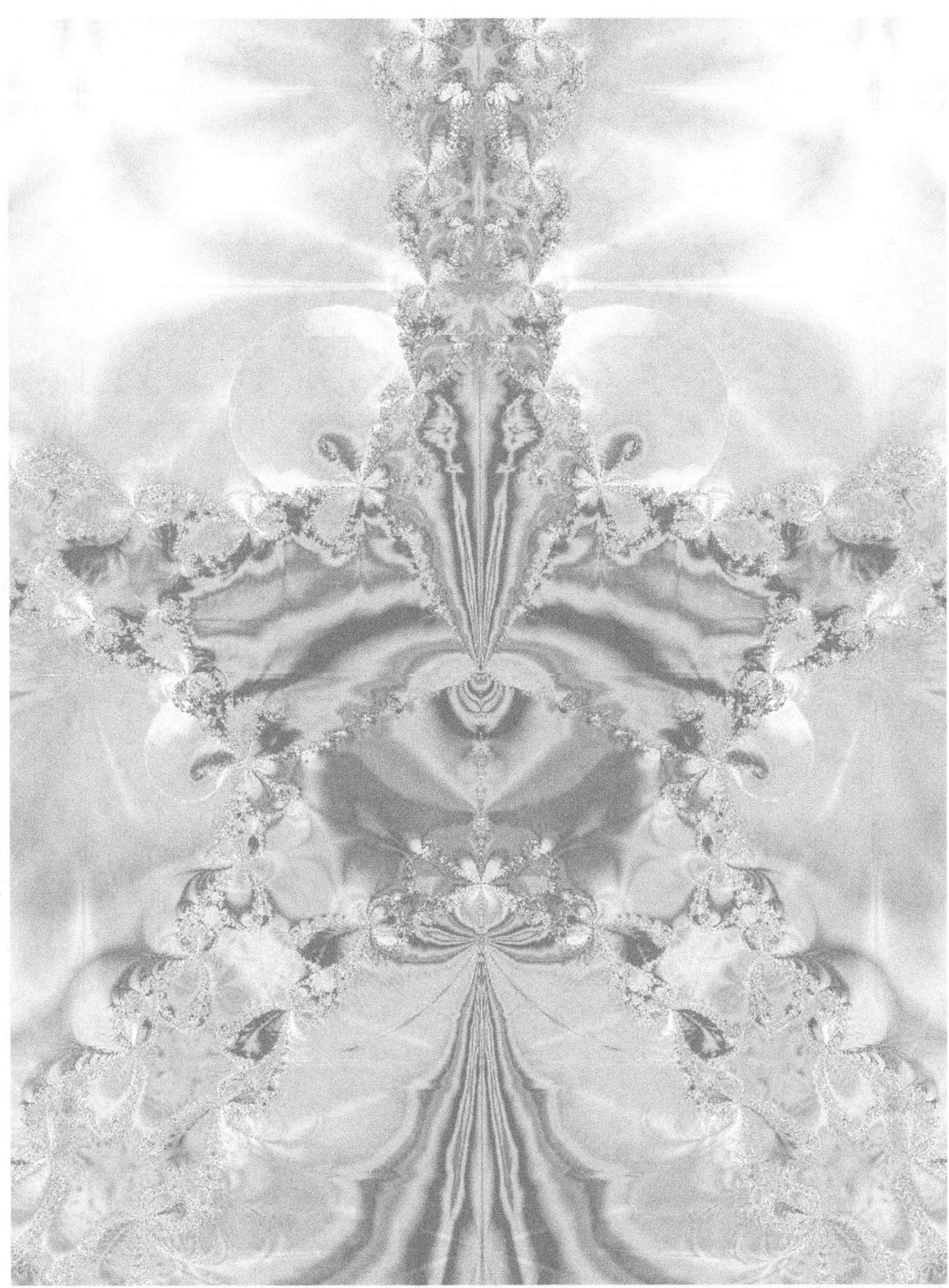

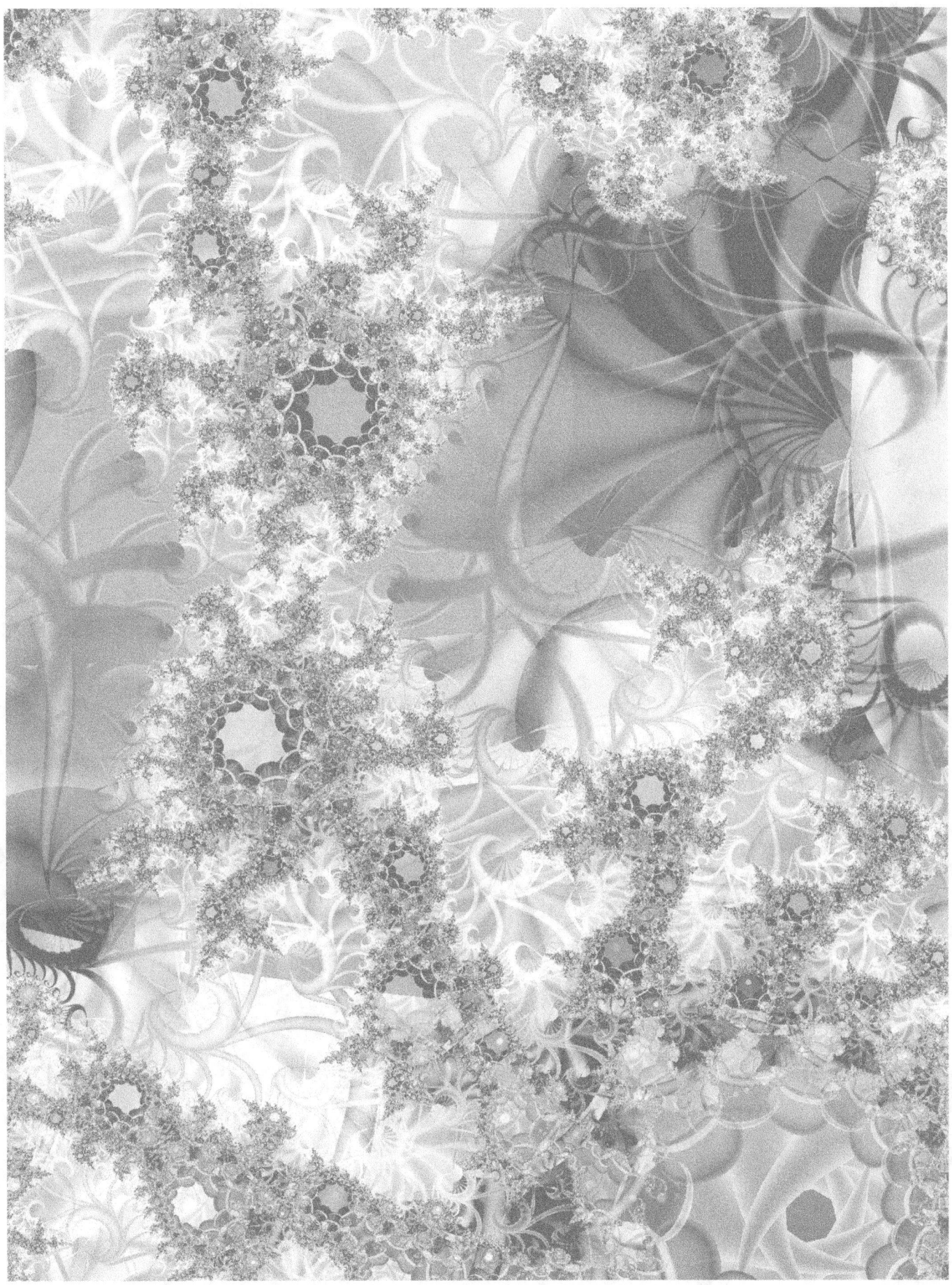

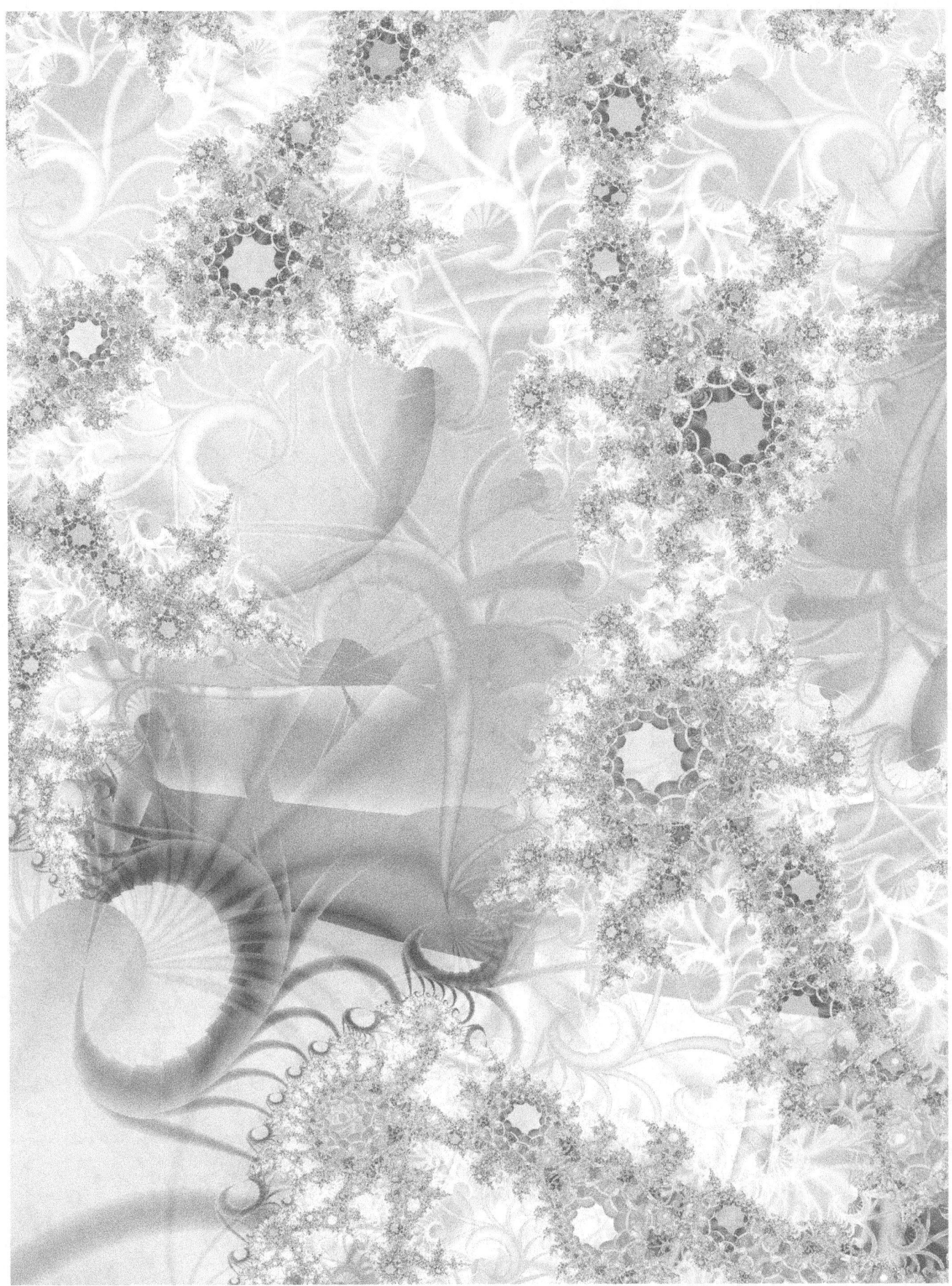

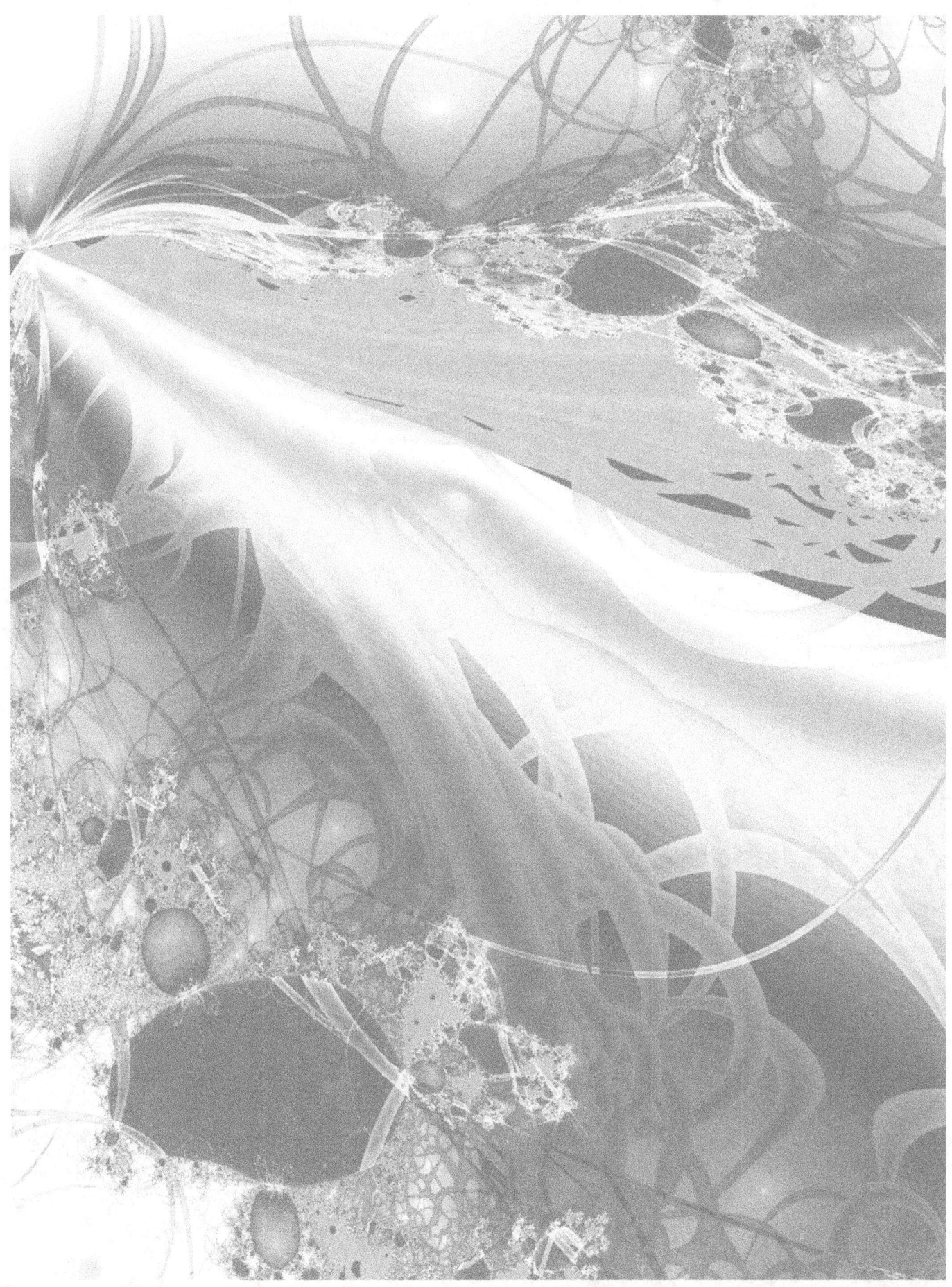

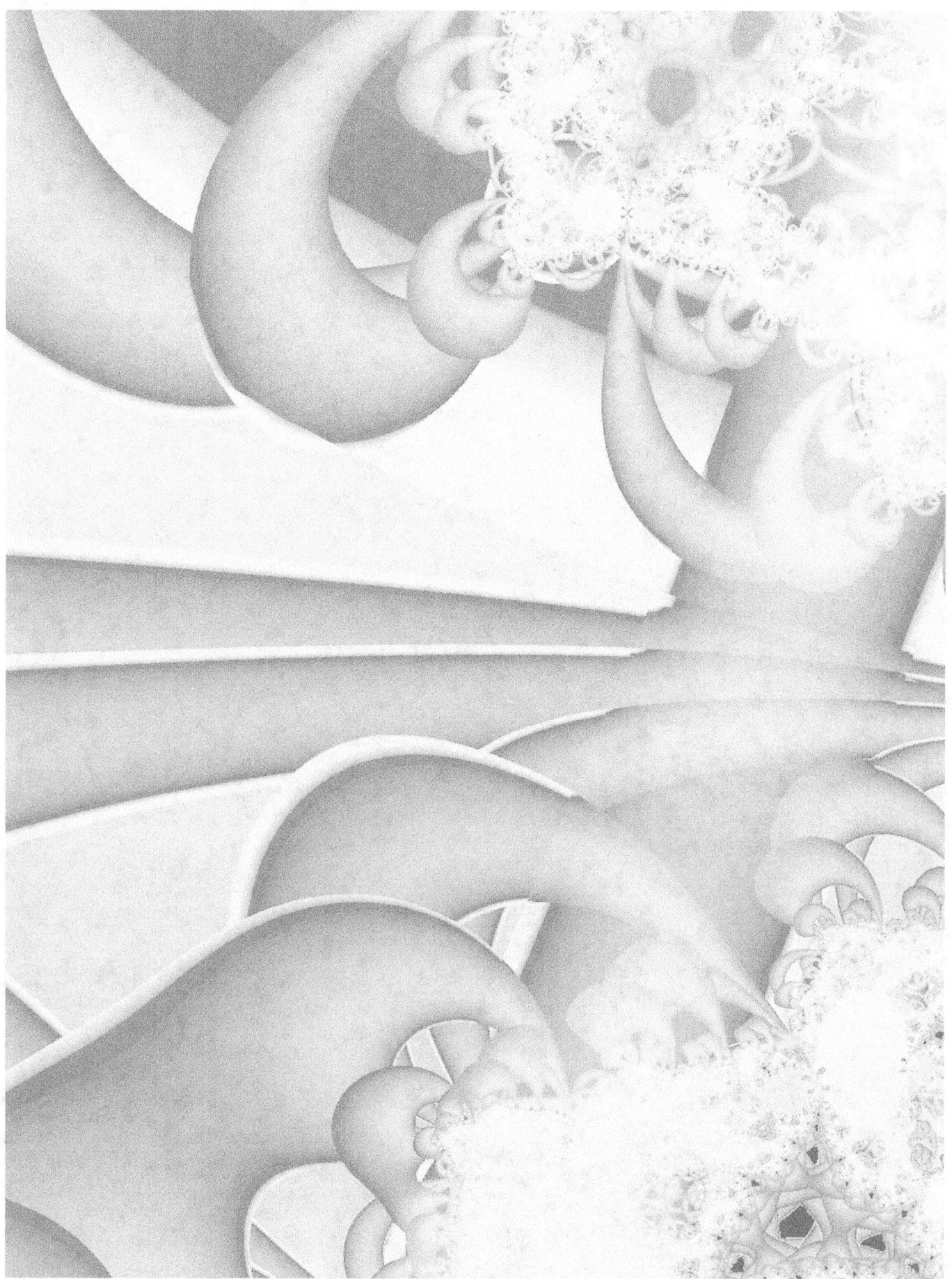

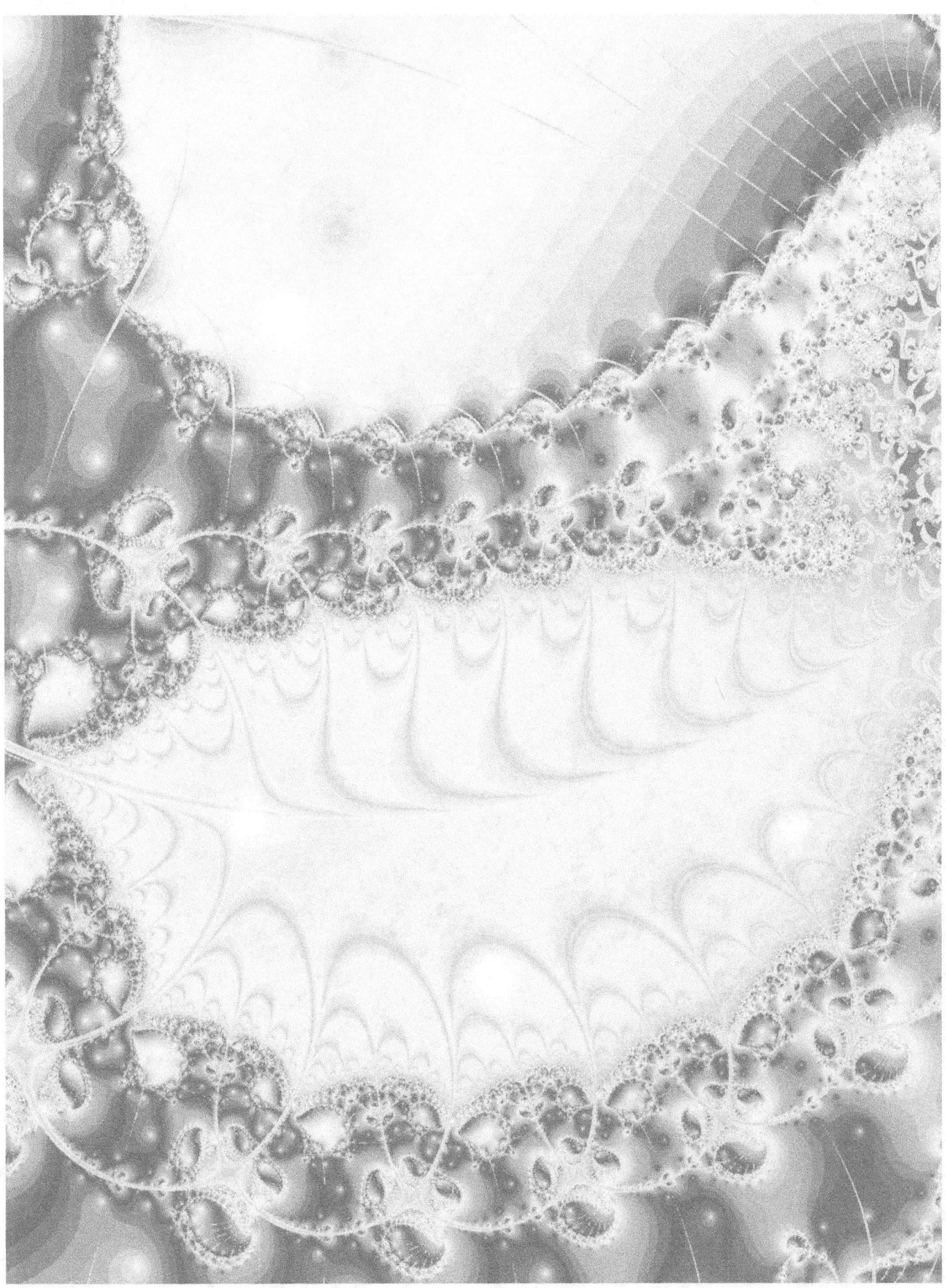

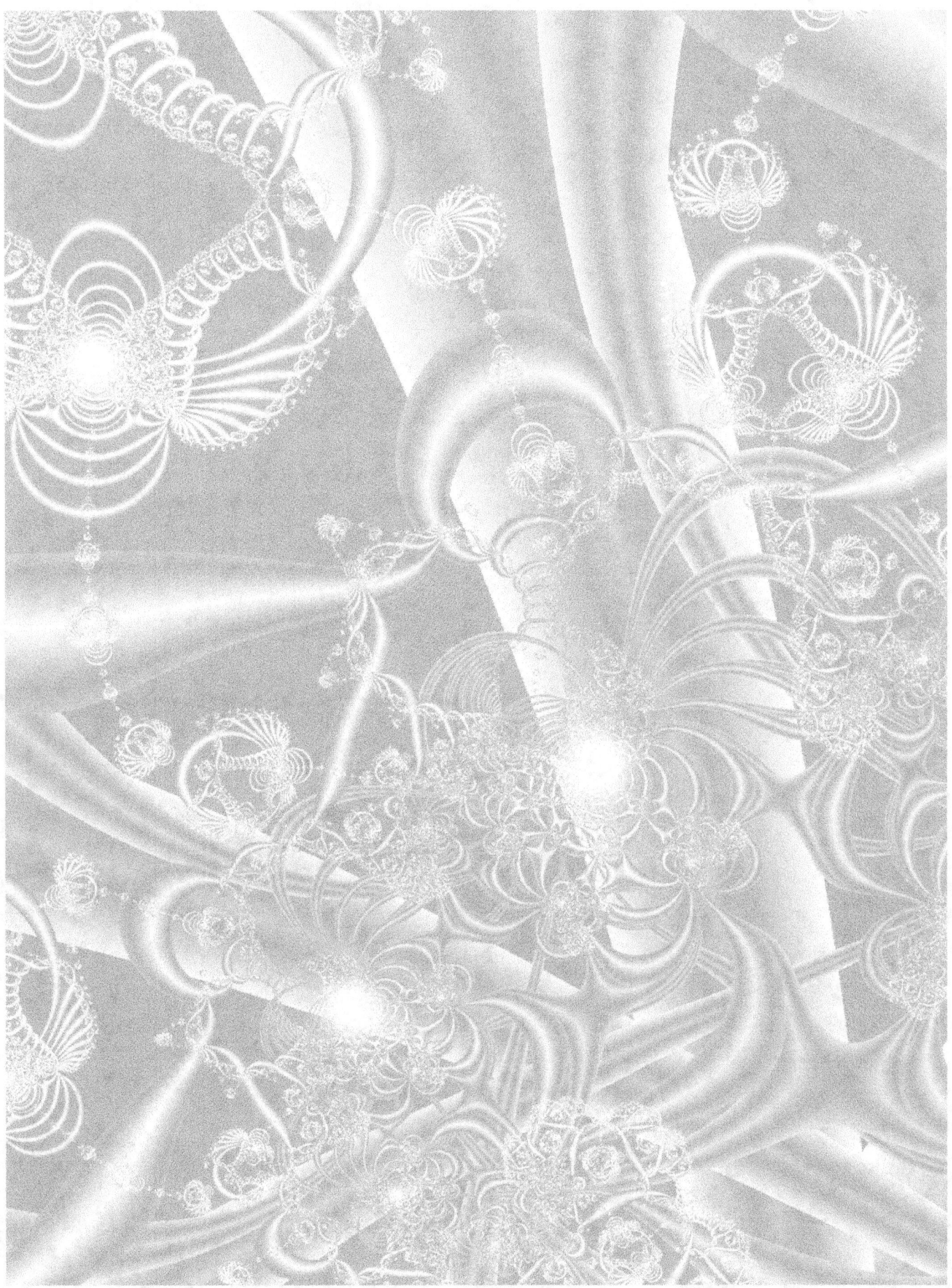

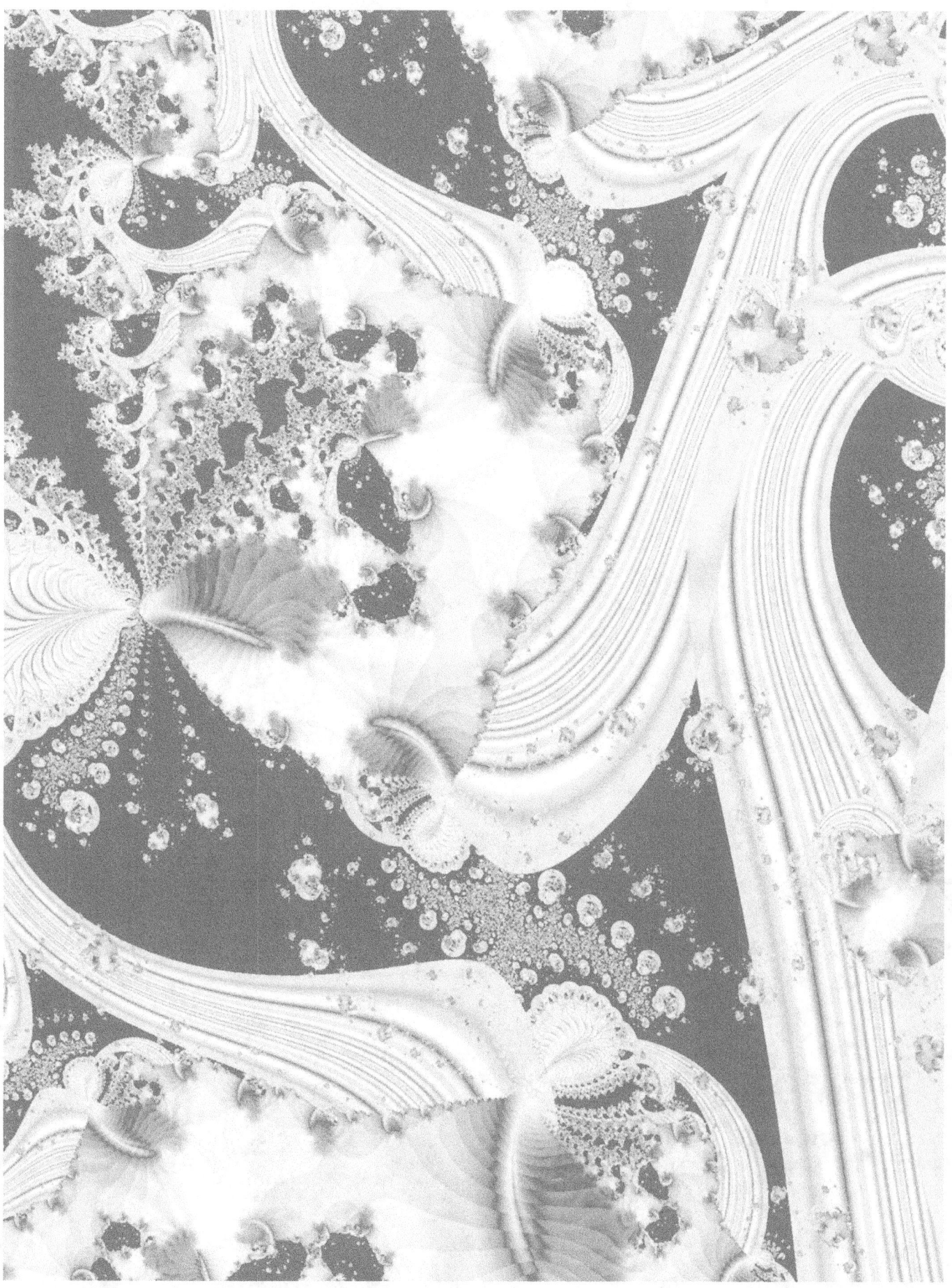

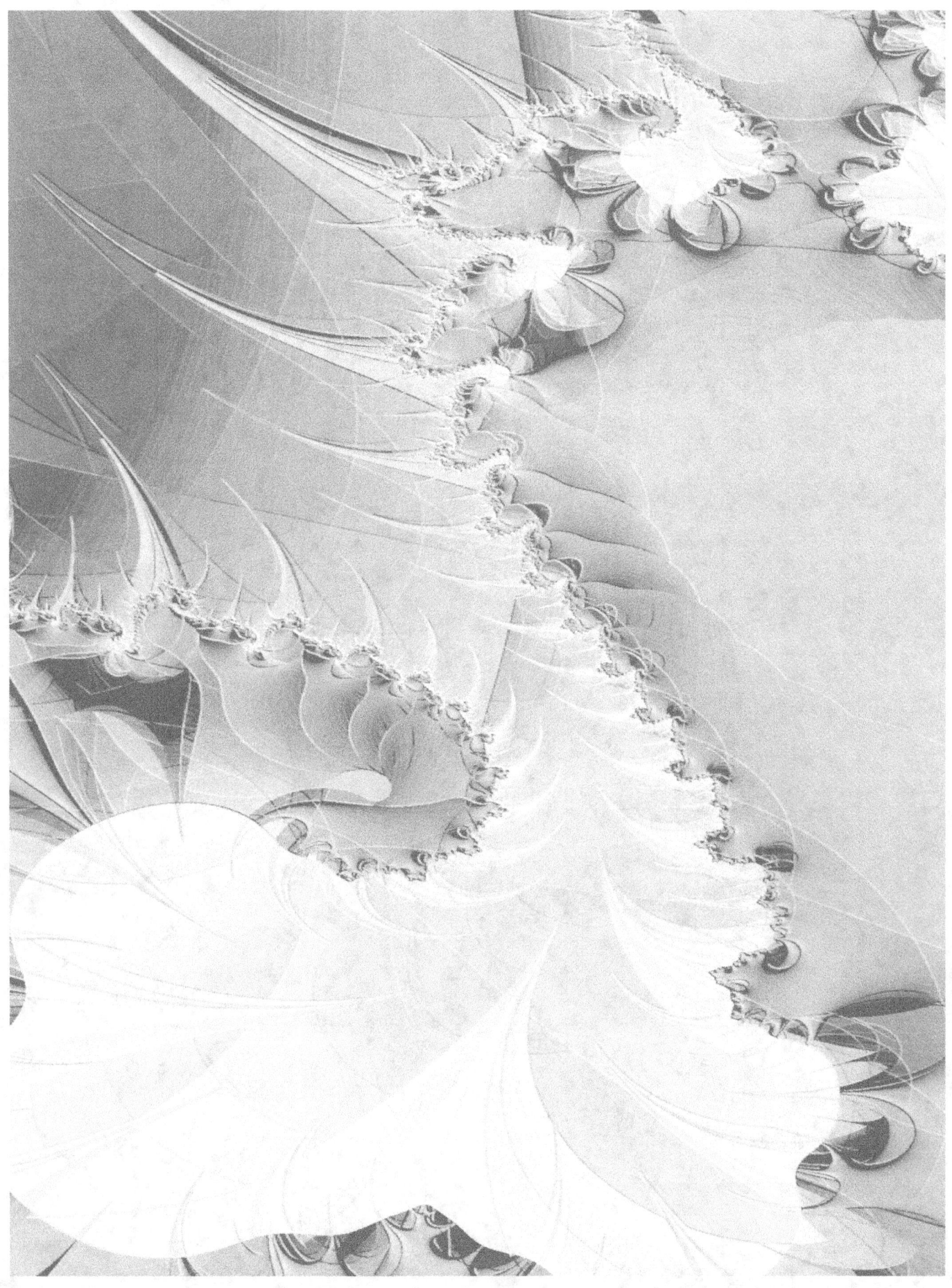

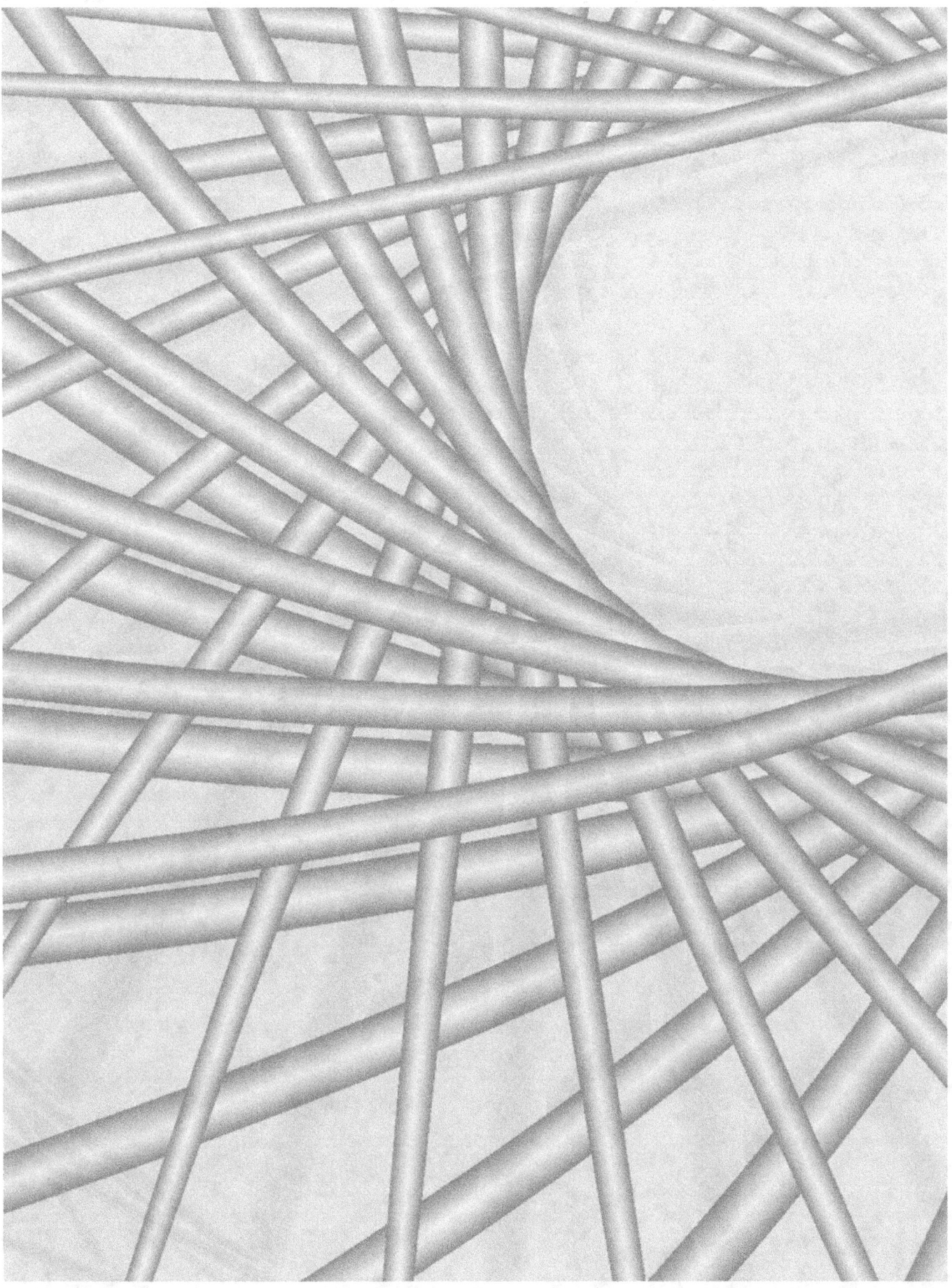

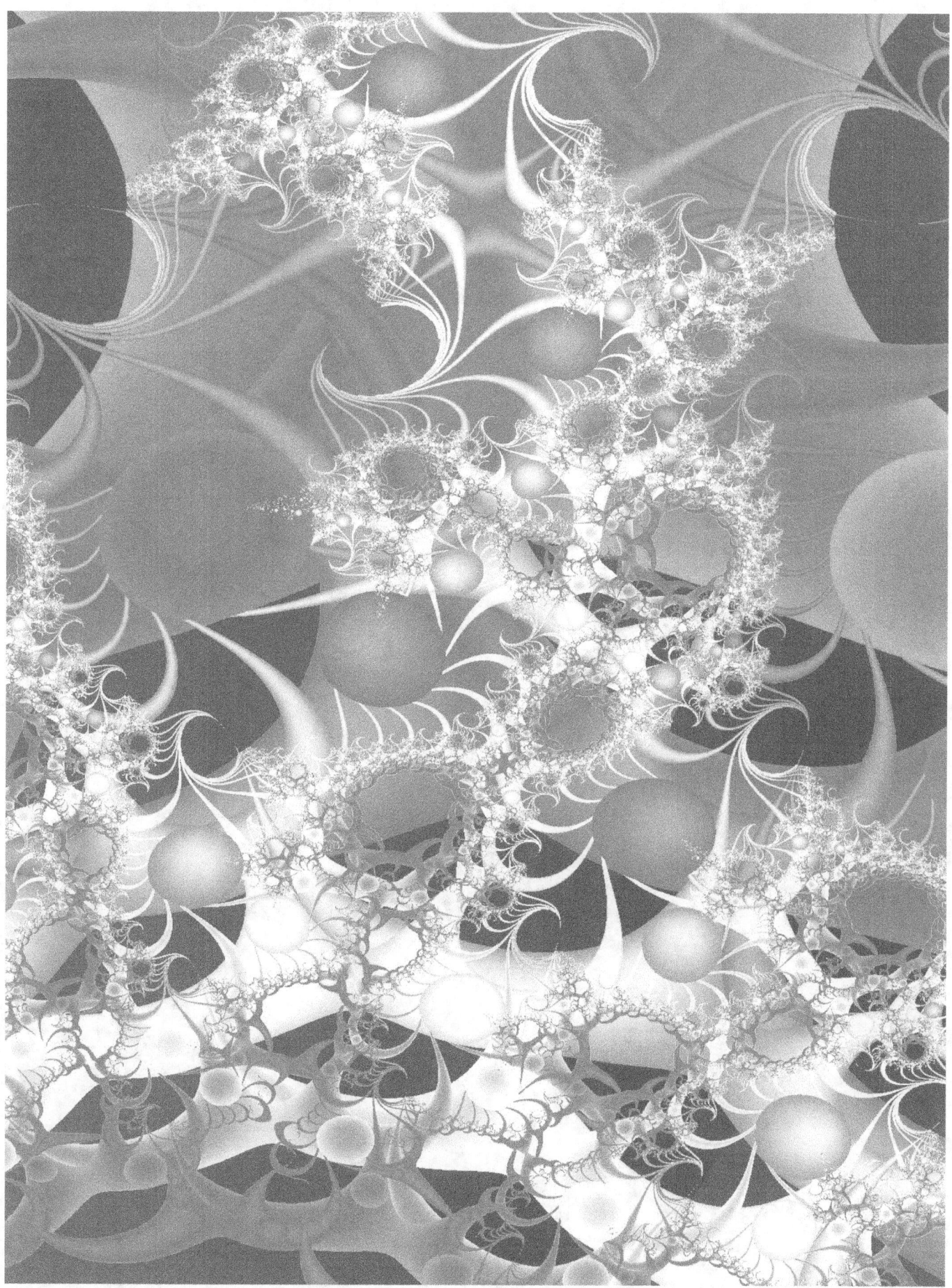

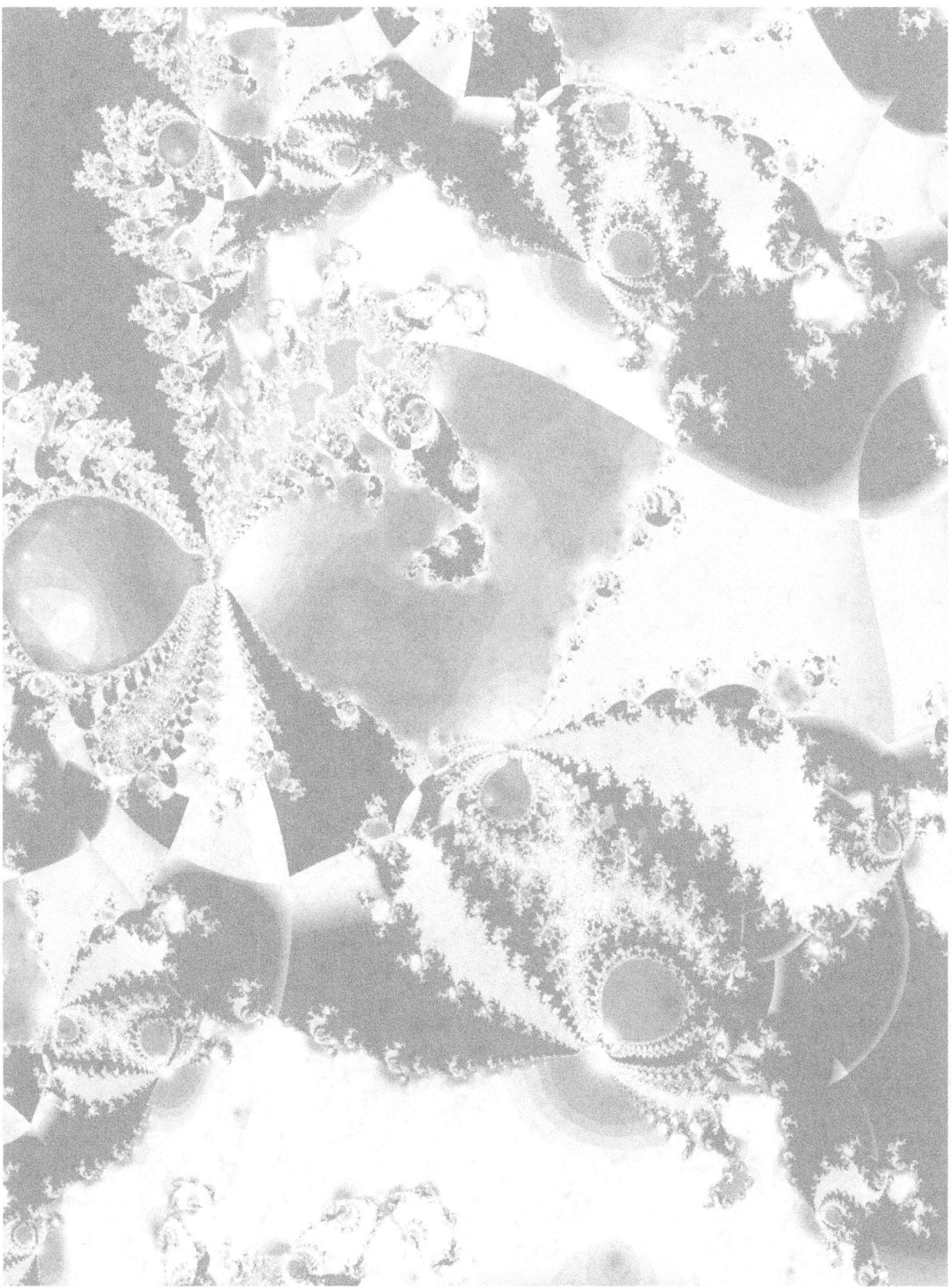

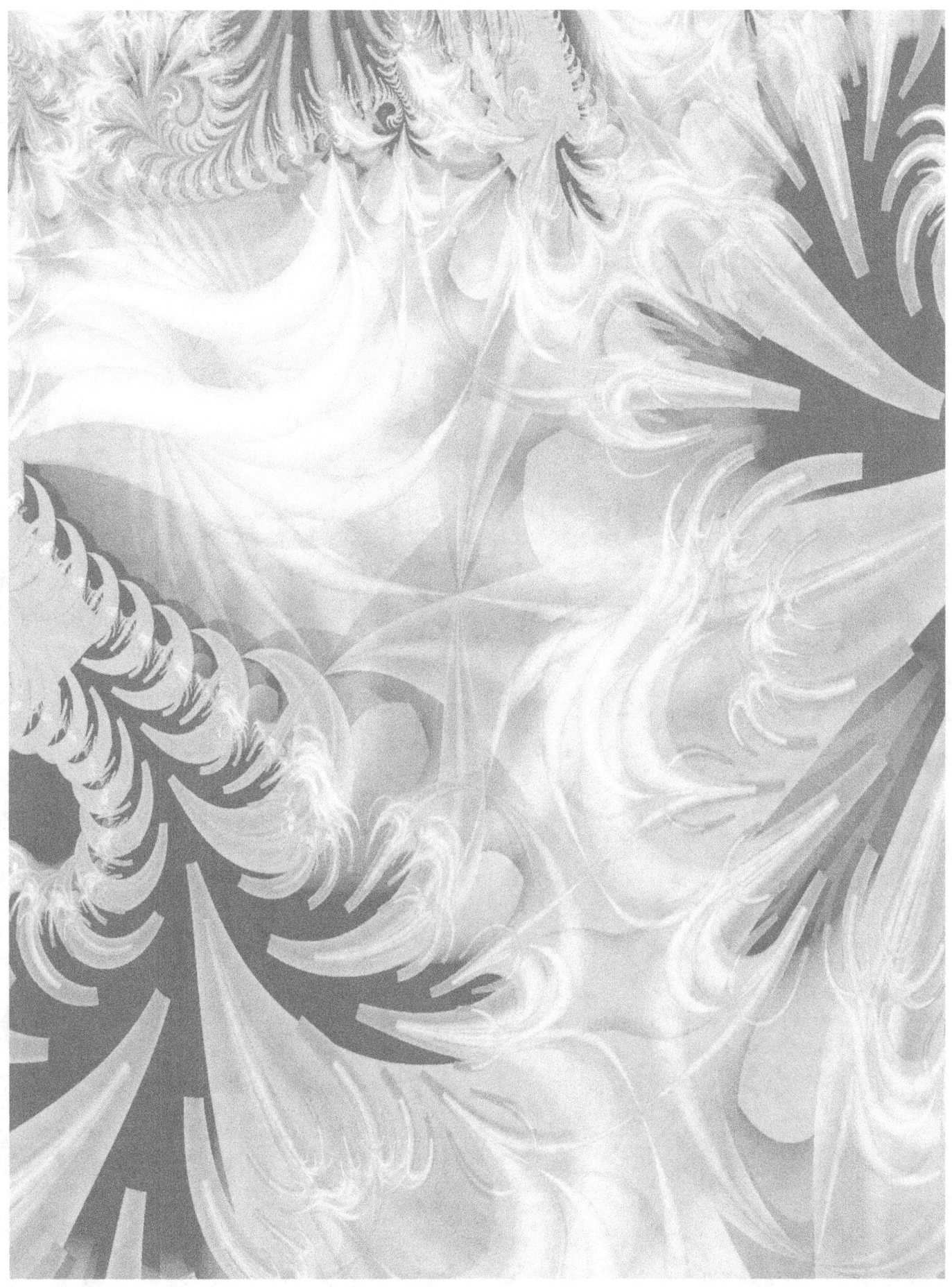

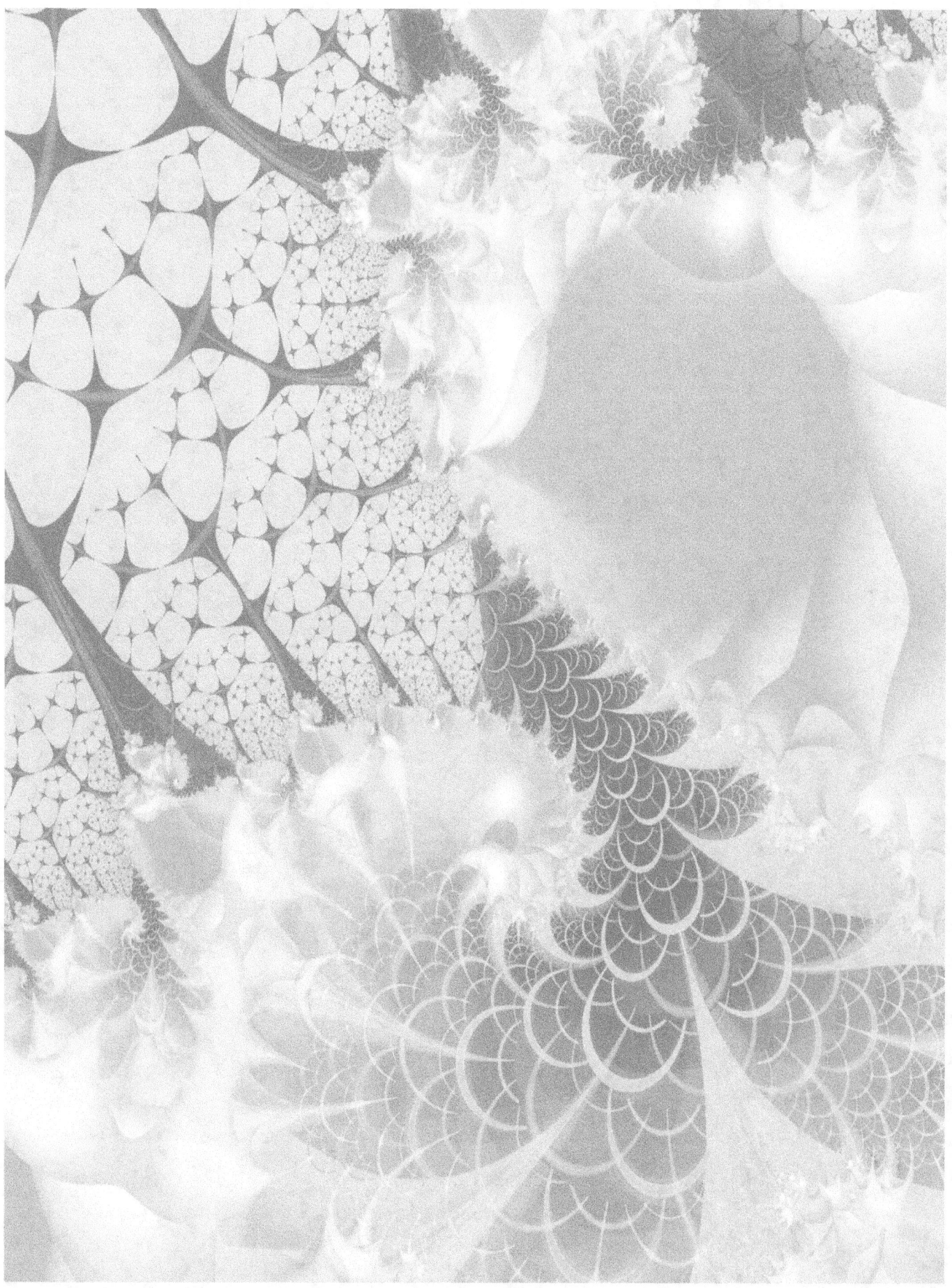

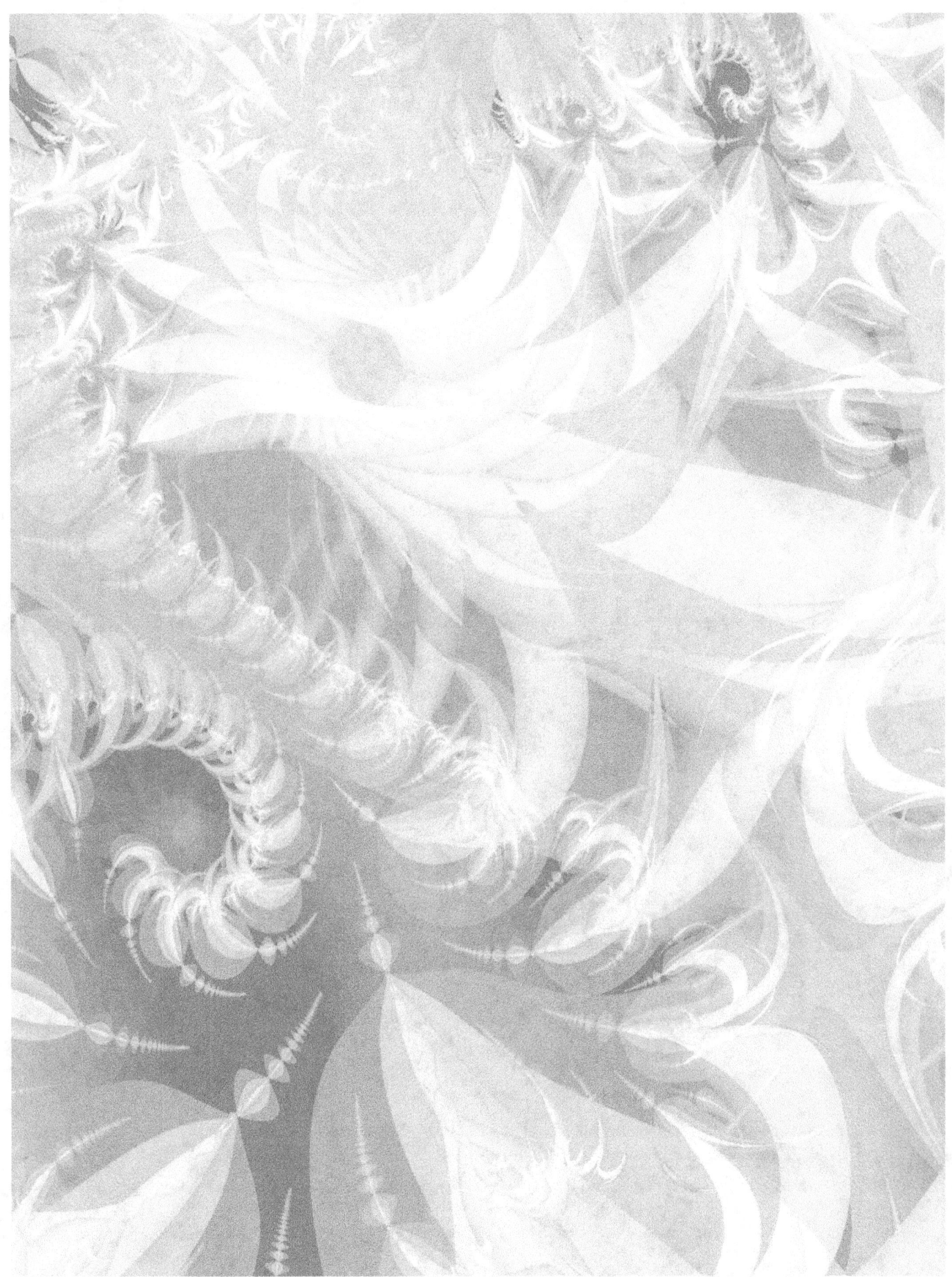

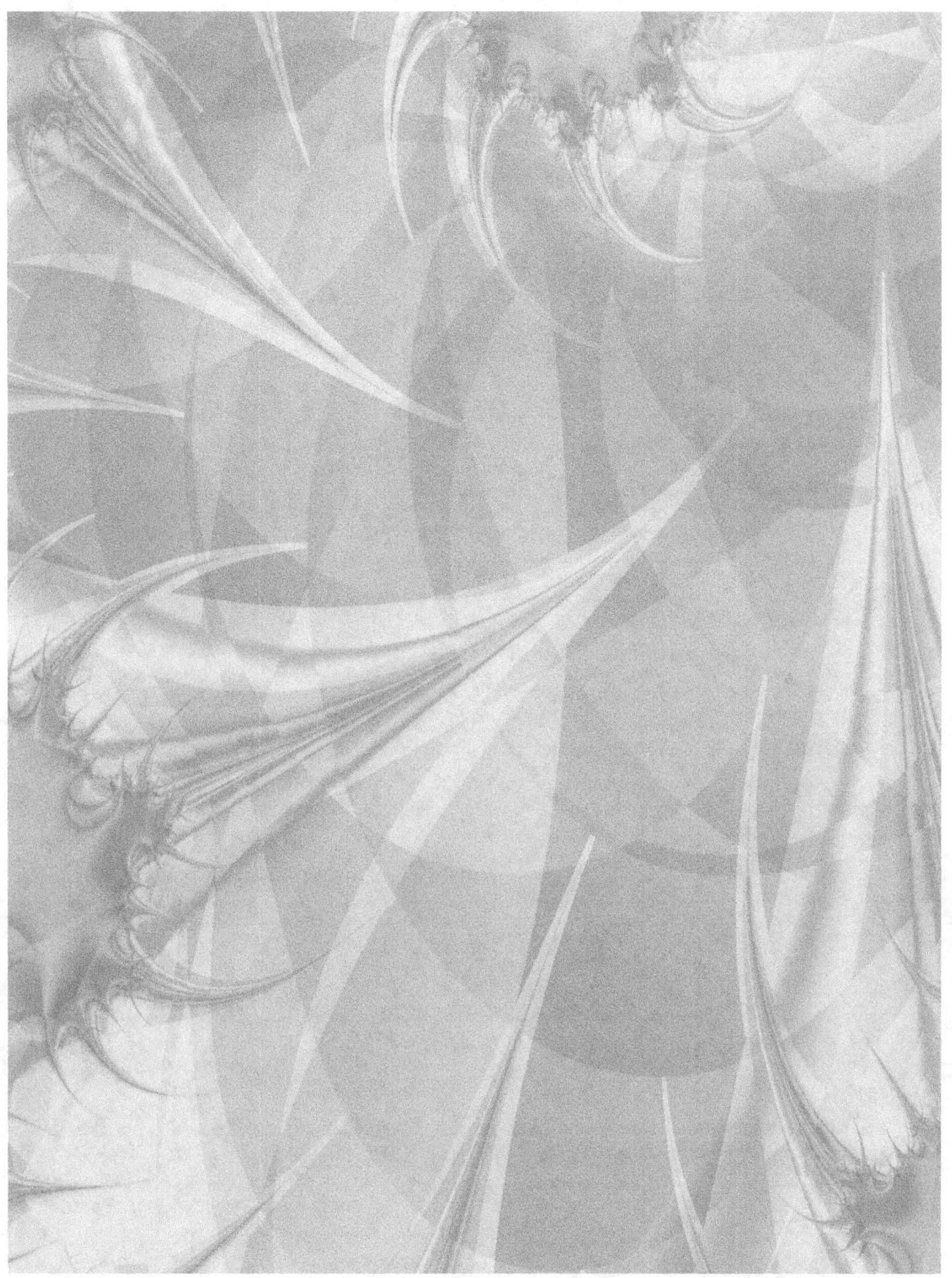

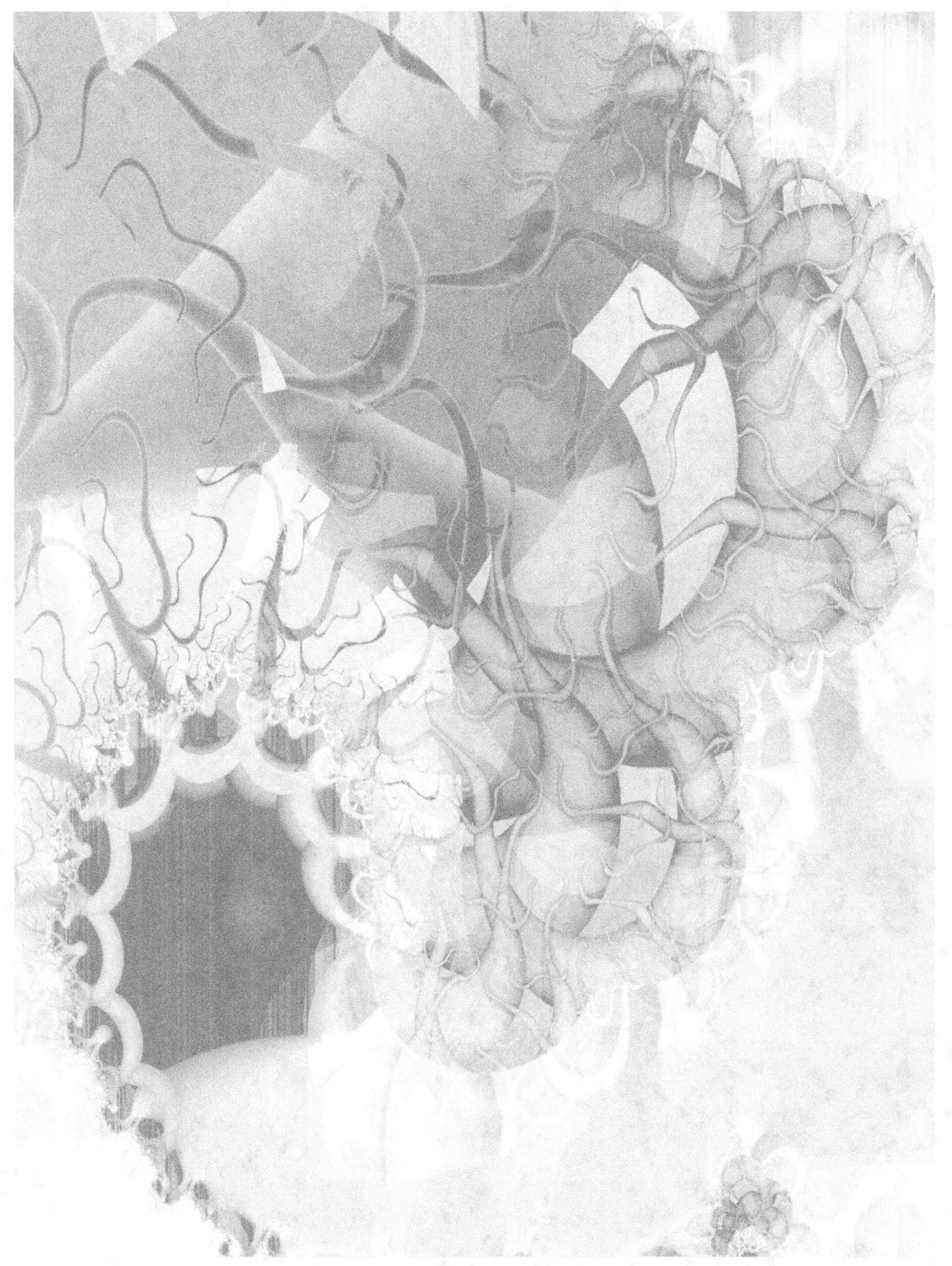

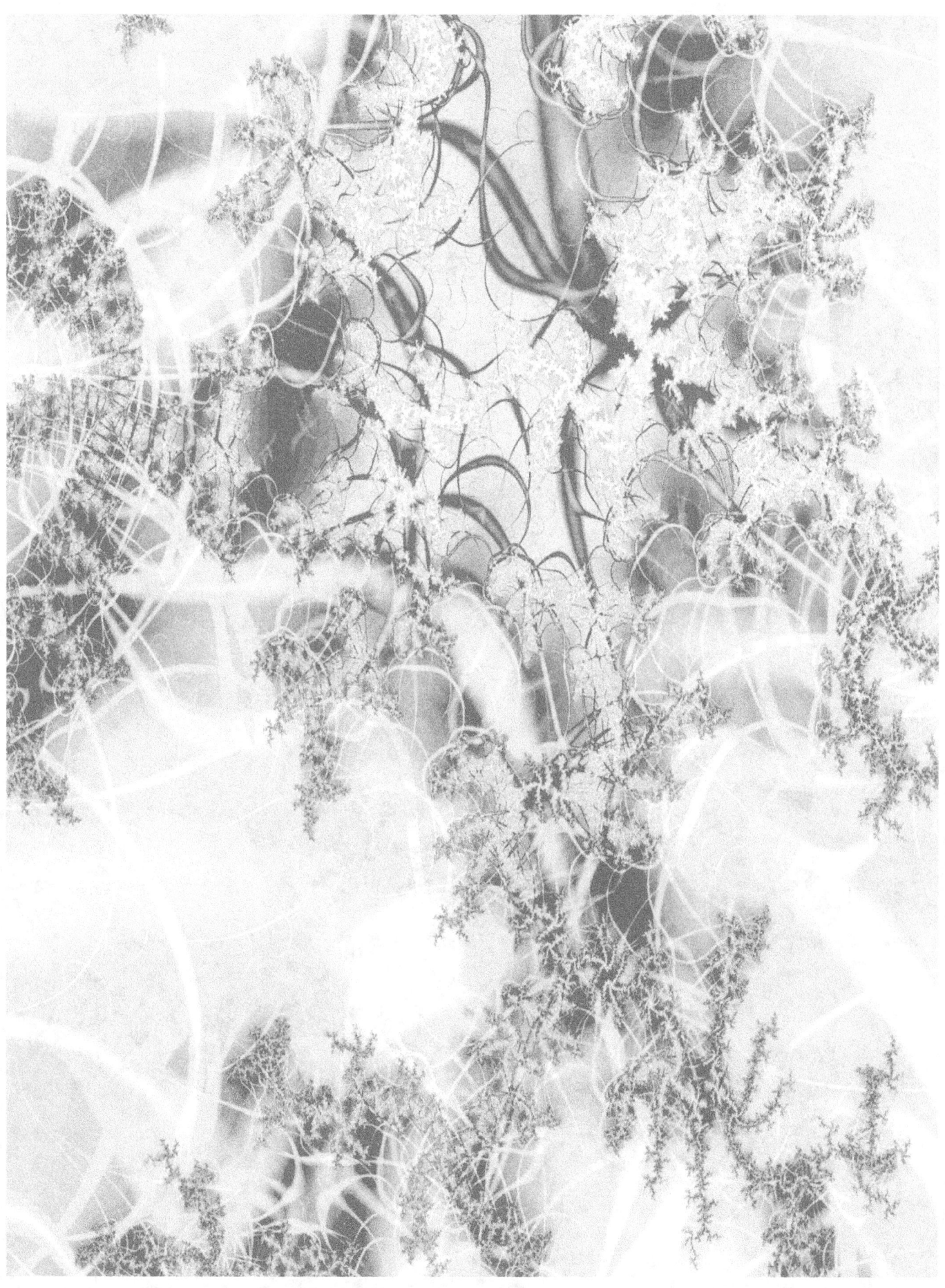

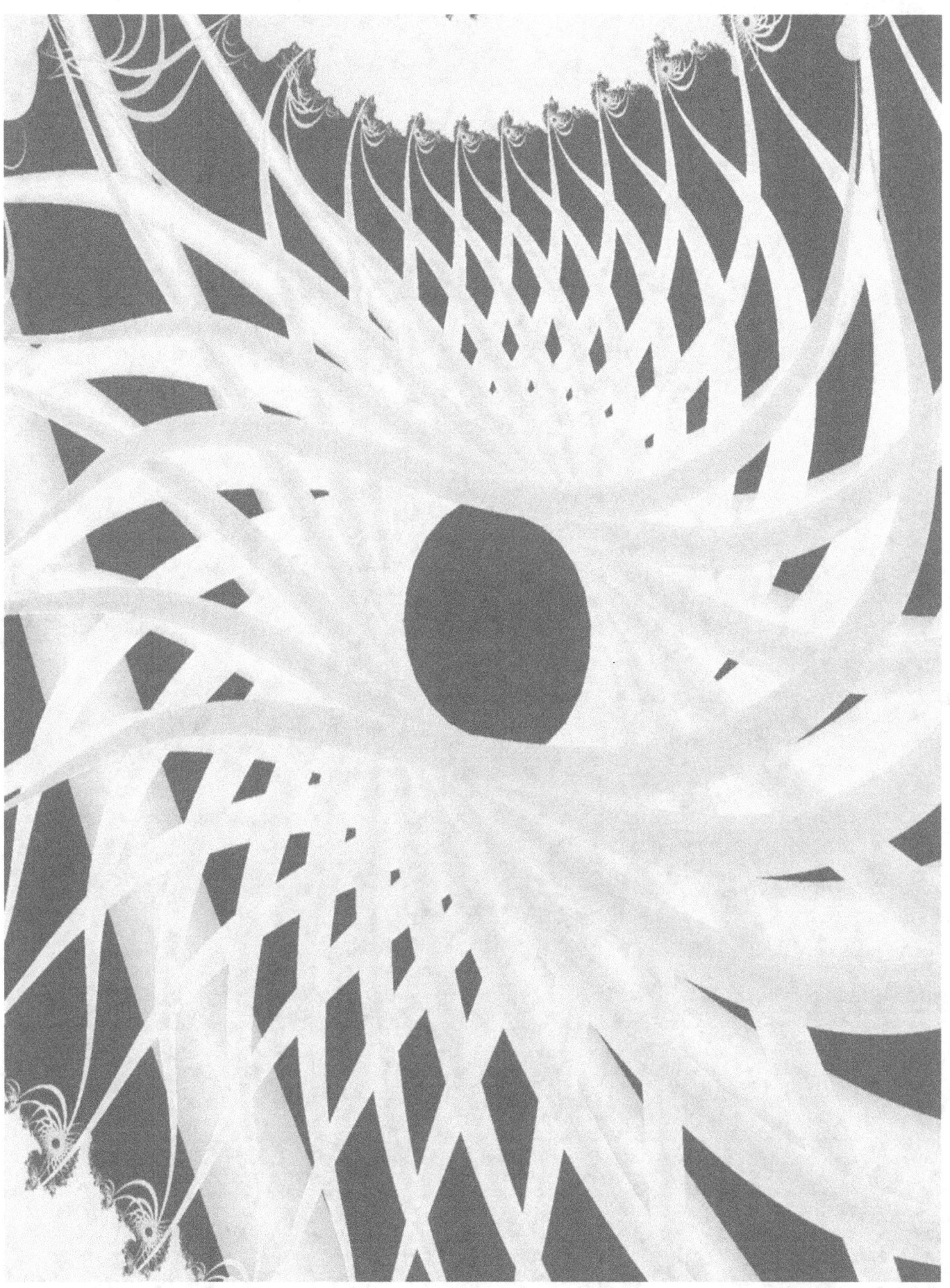

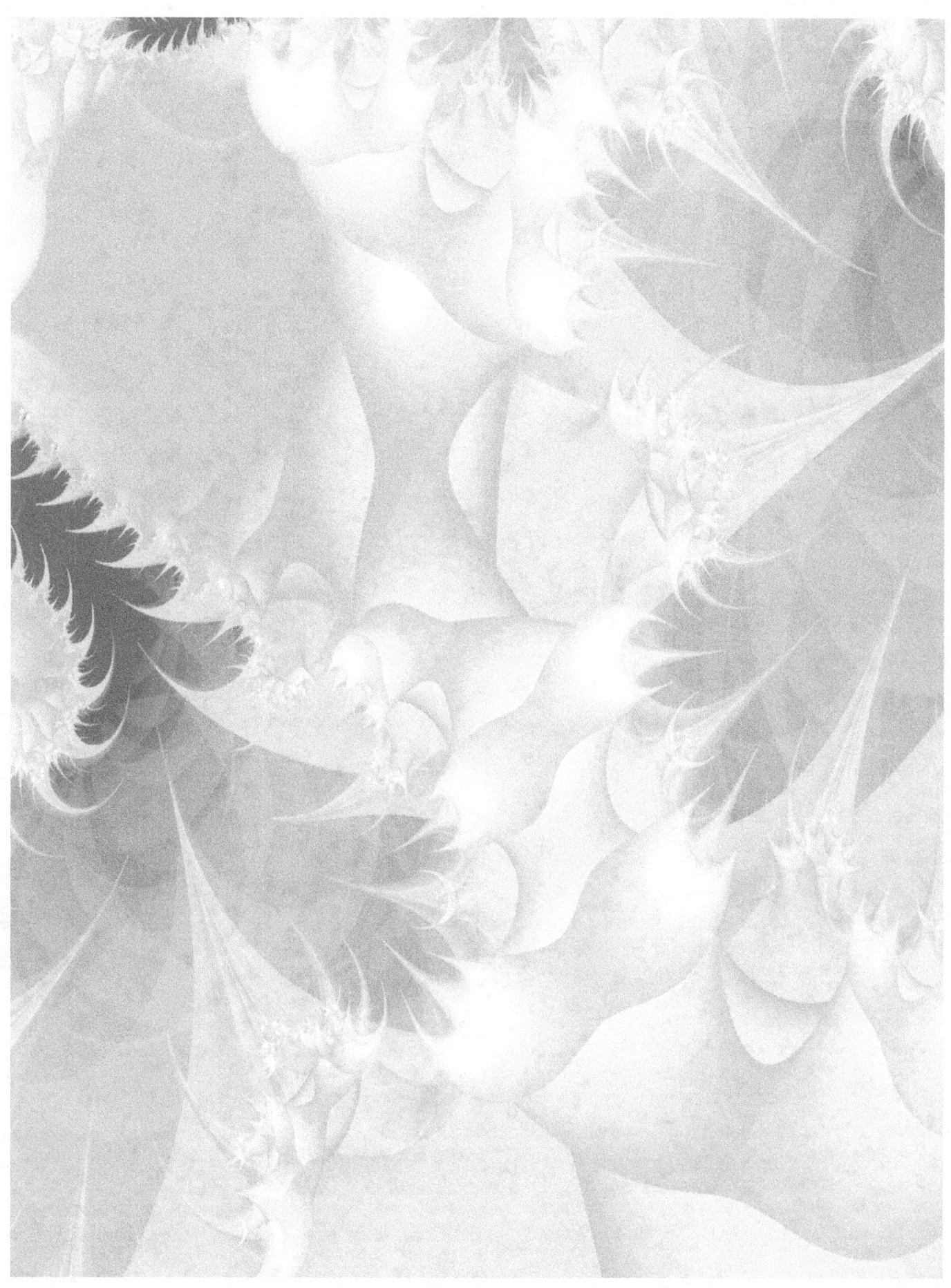

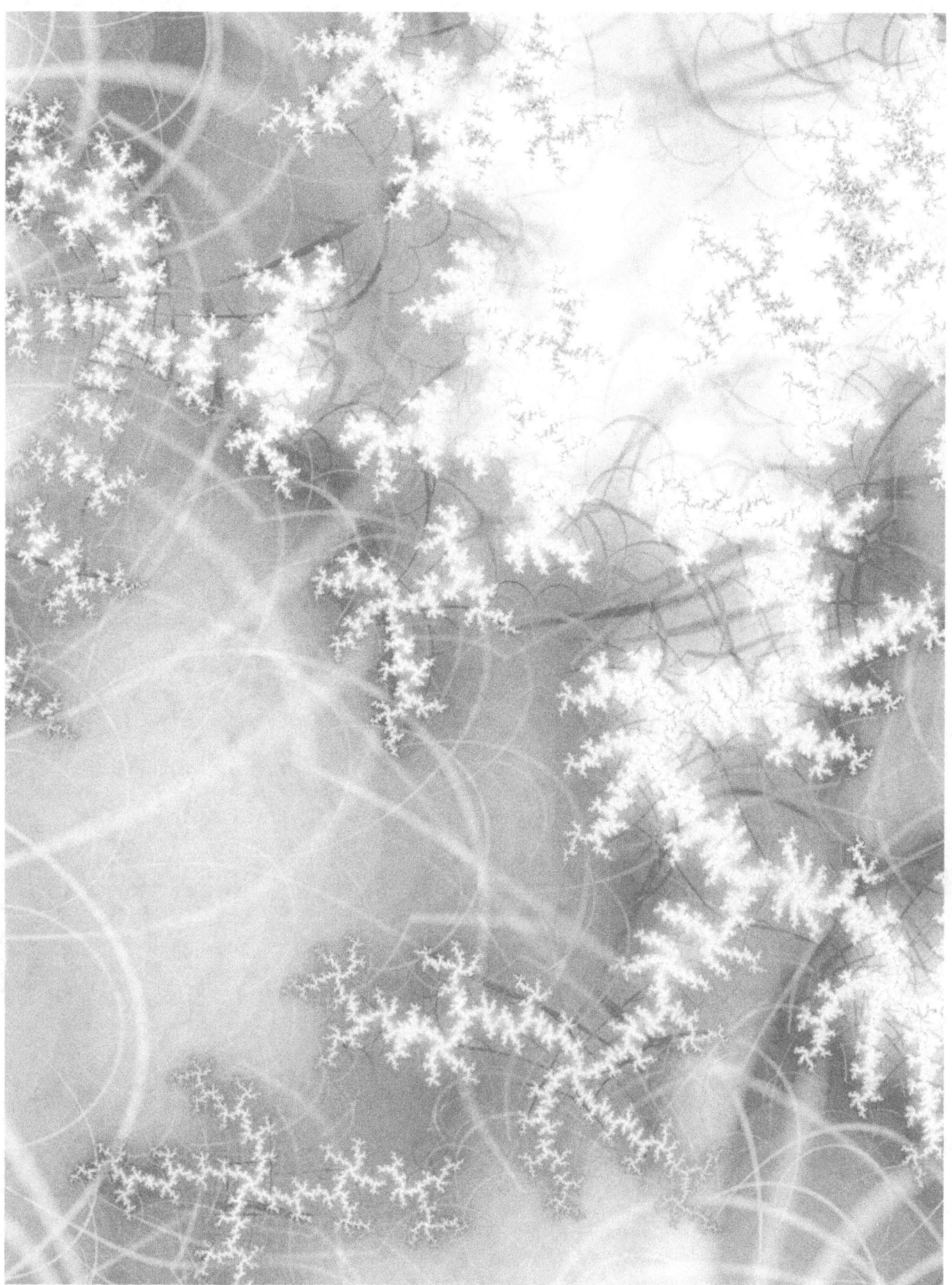

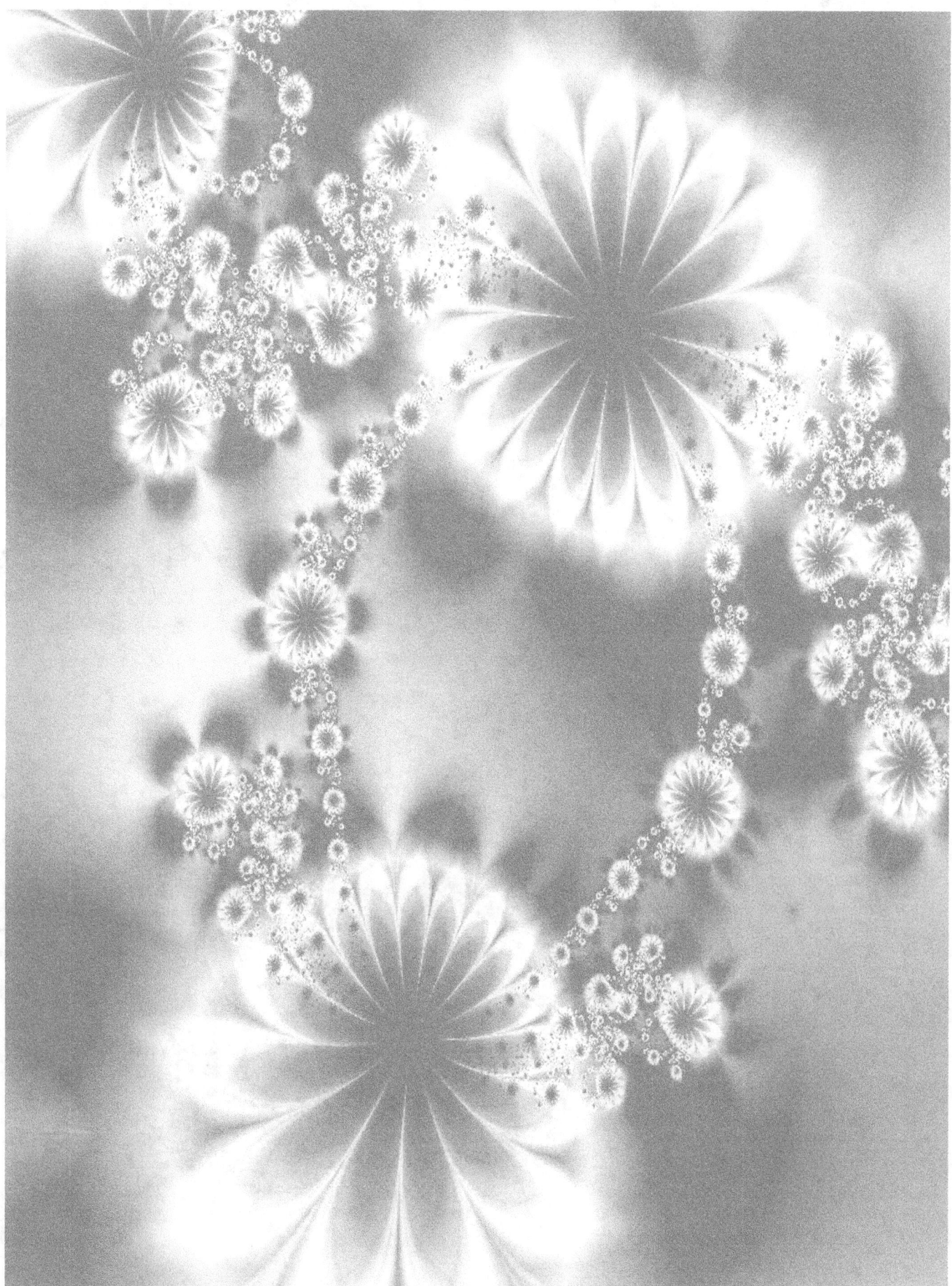

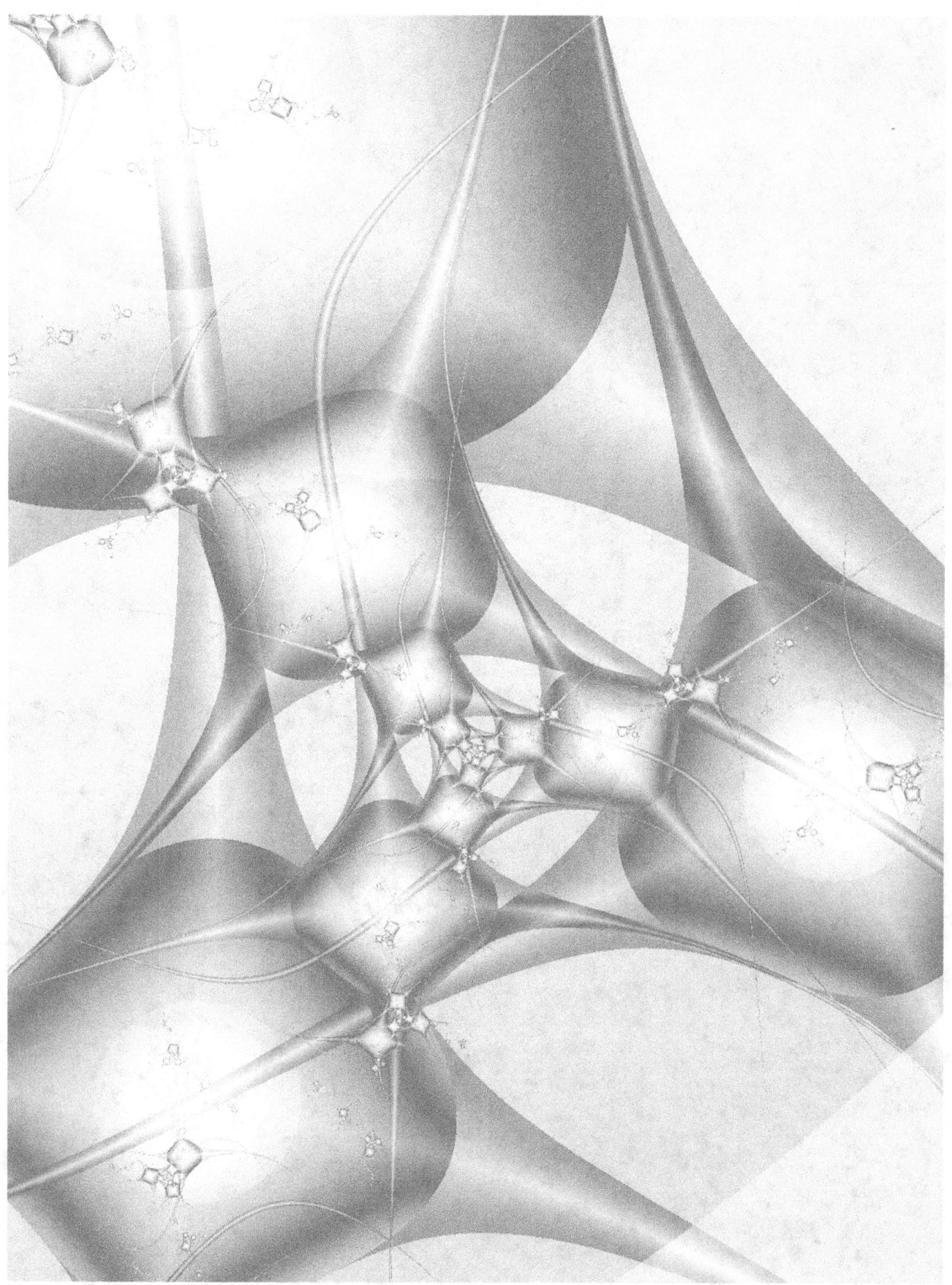

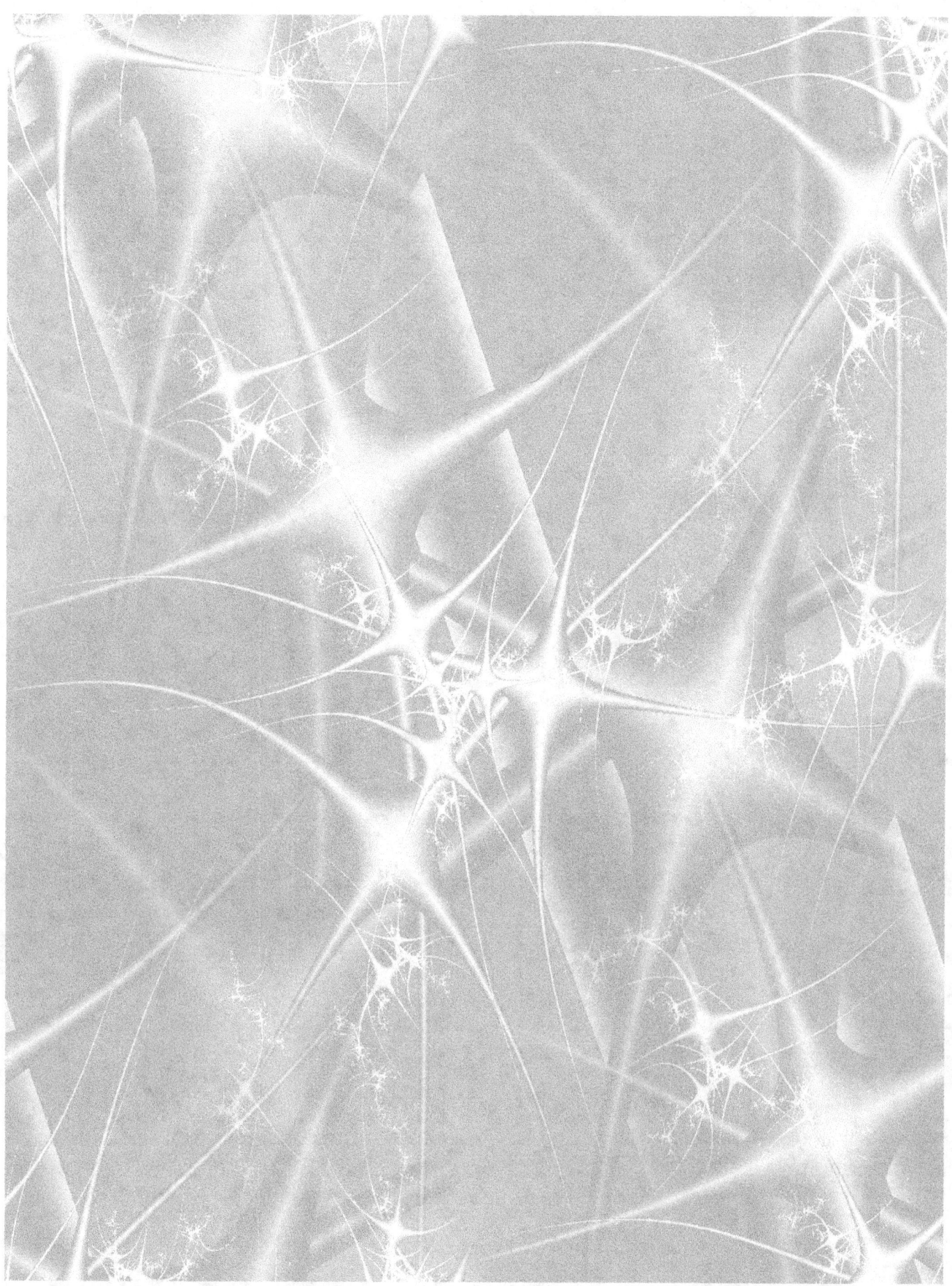

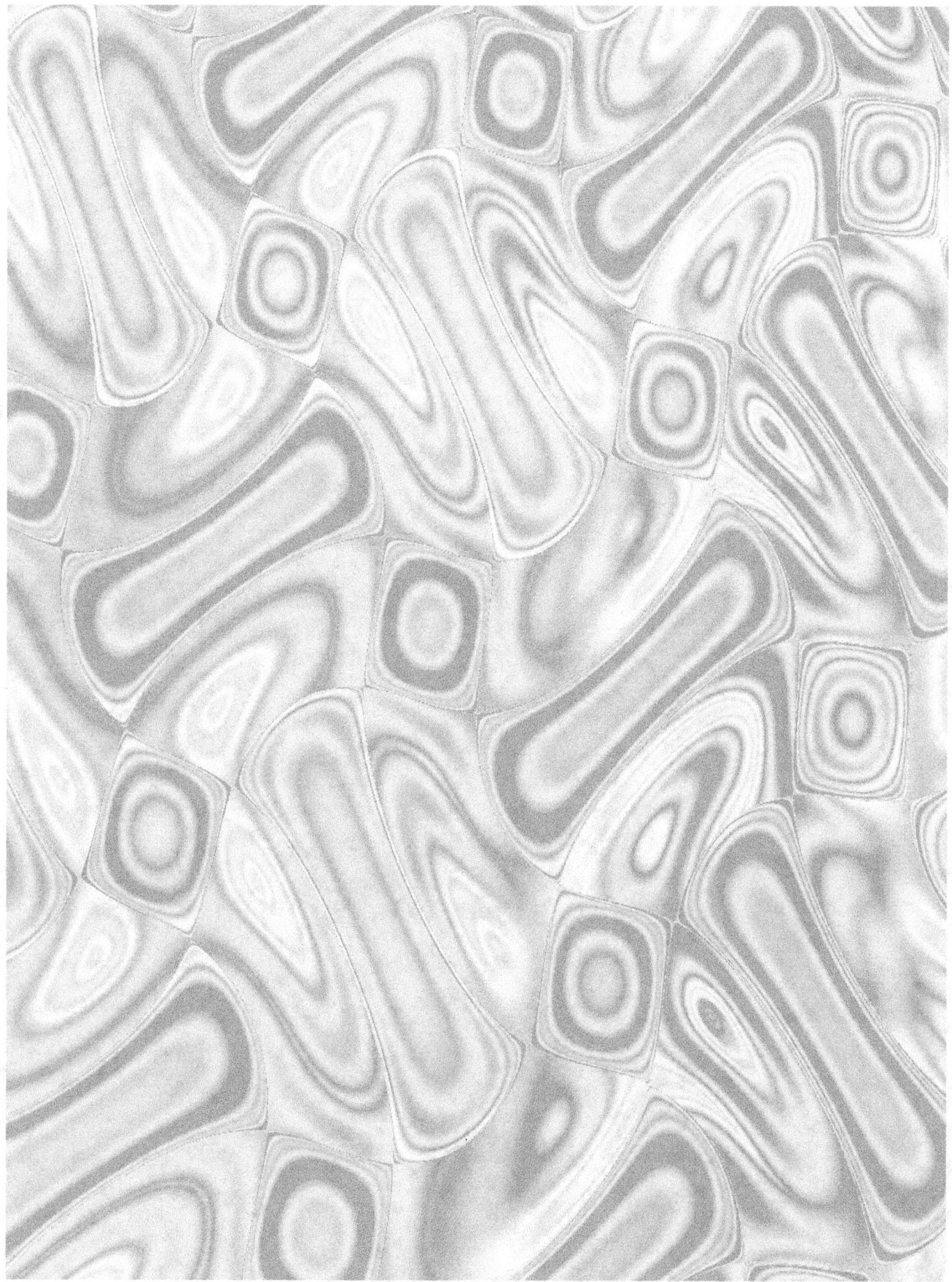

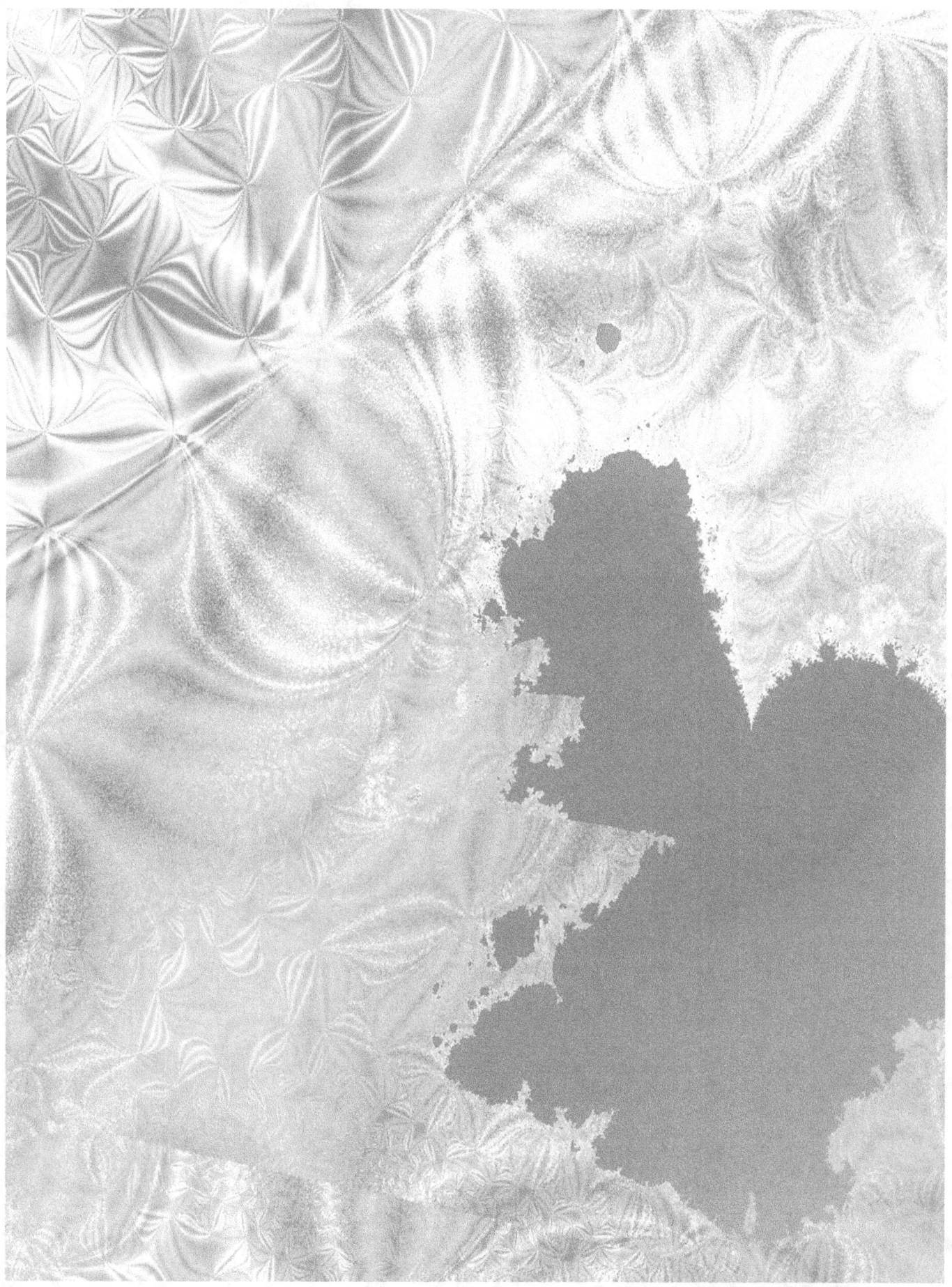

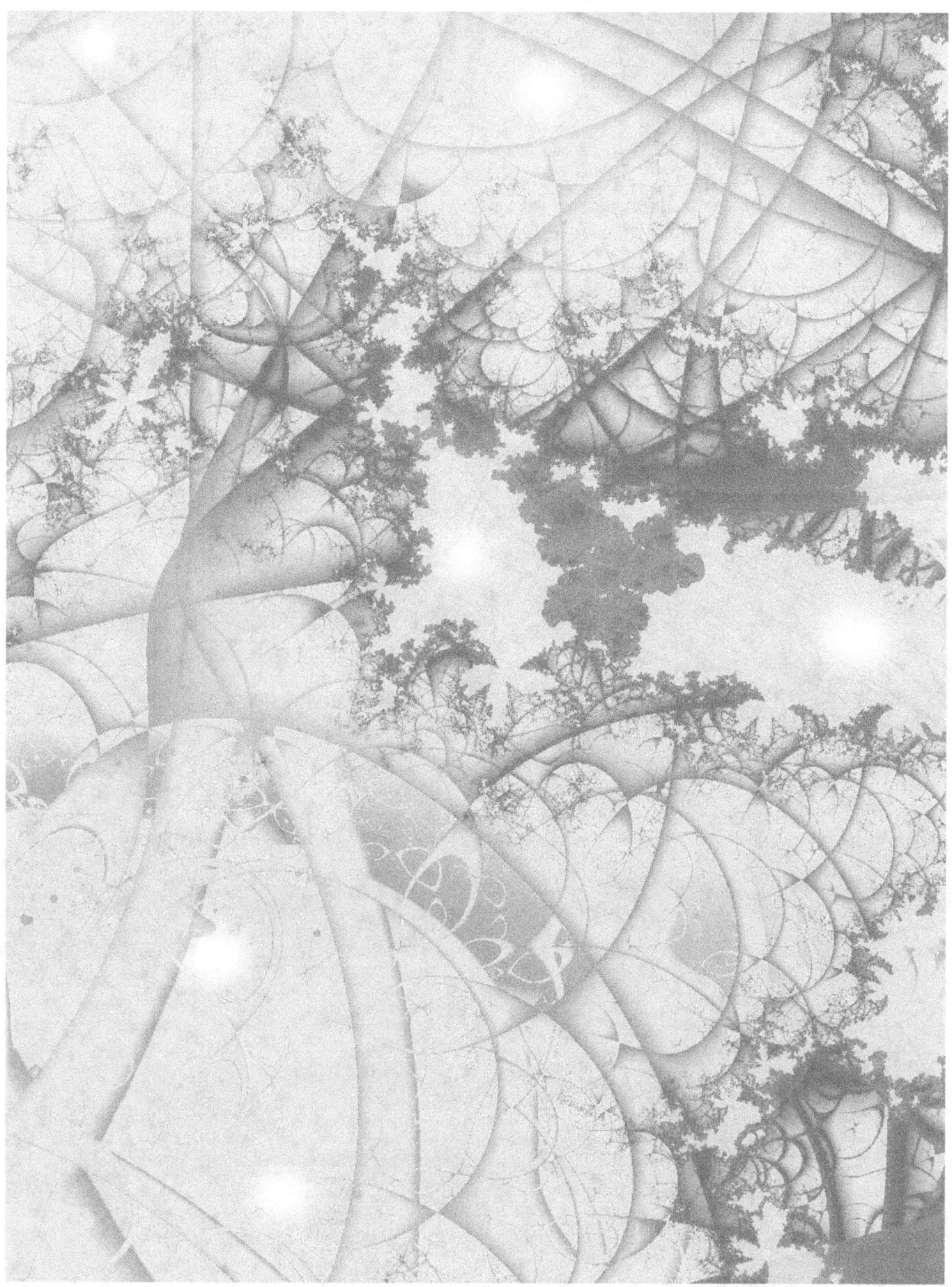

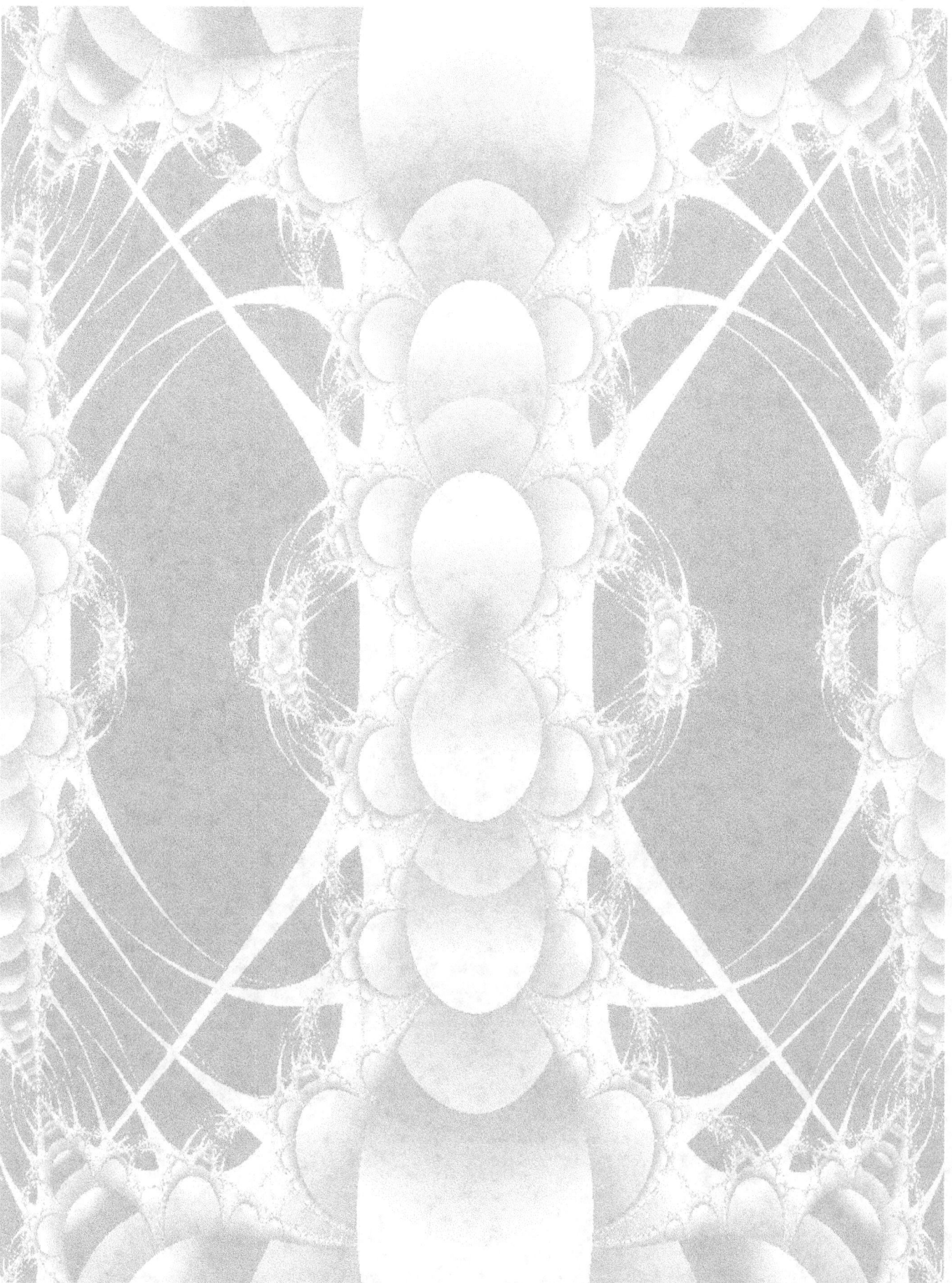

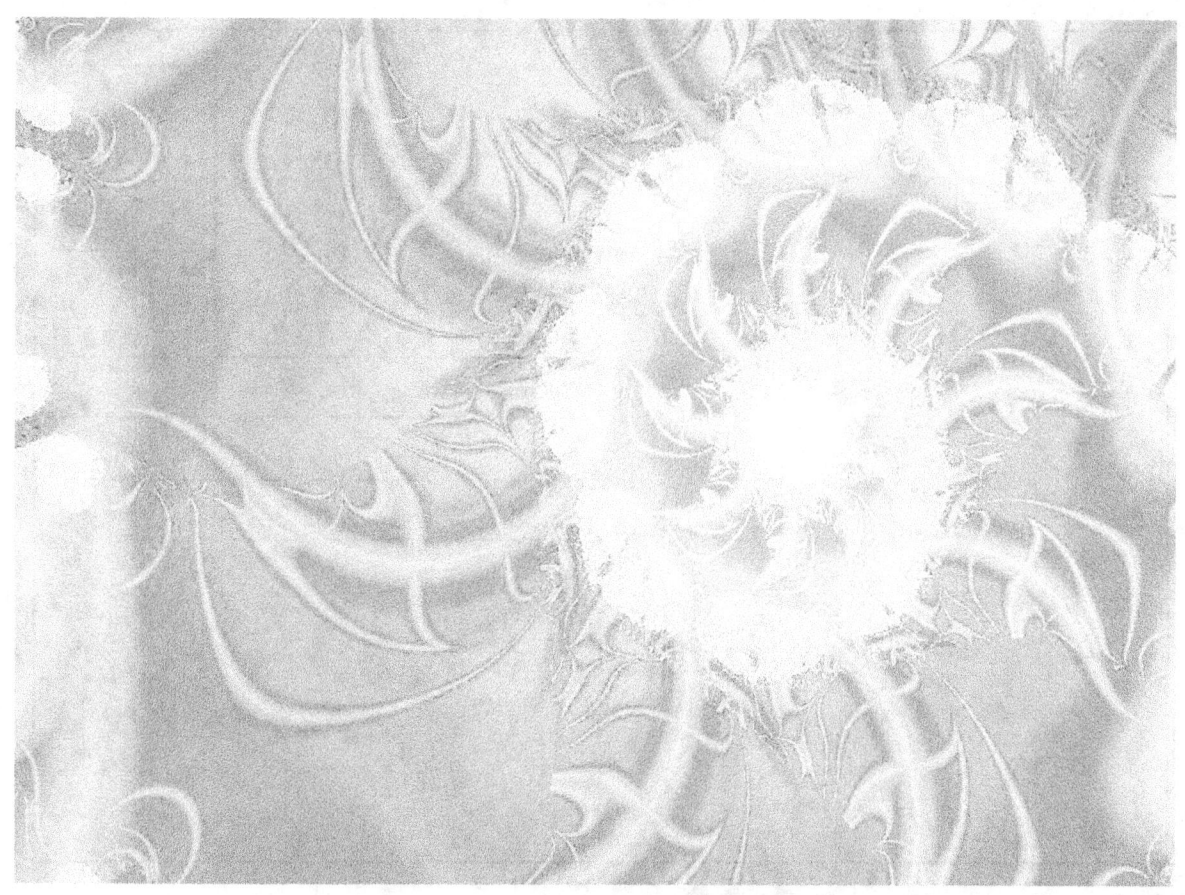

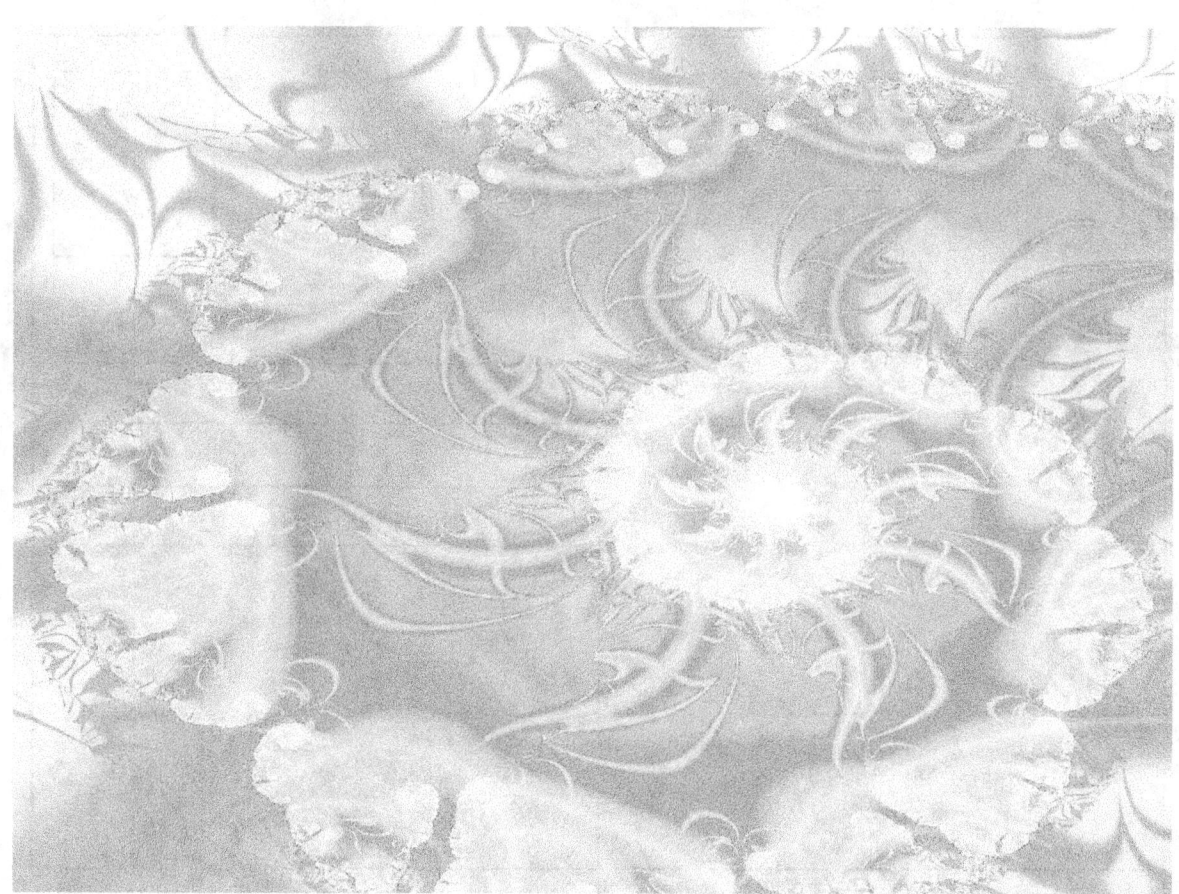

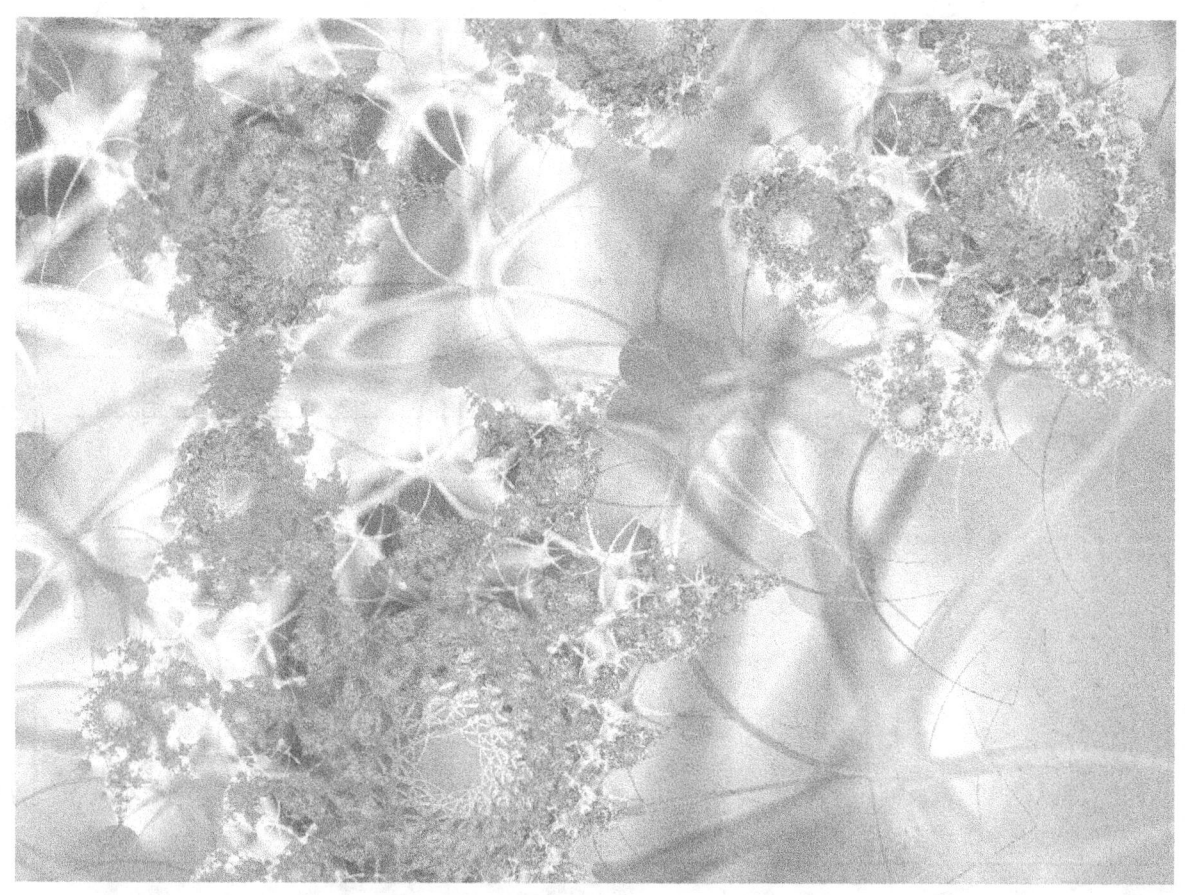

ABOUT THE AUTHOR

Hannah Moesker is dedicated to publishing high-resolution grayscale coloring books with a sophisticated look and feel for adults.

Mrs. Moesker works traditionally in pen and ink, markers, colored pencils, gel pens and pastel chalk, as well as digitally in making fractal art and (name)mandala's.

She lives in the Netherlands with her husband, son and a lot of birds.